A Sacred Thirst for Liberty

By
Frederick Douglass

PADMORE PUBLISHING GROUP

A Sacred Thirst for Liberty Editing, Research and Additional Writing: Angela Mosley © 2016 All rights reserved. Printed in the United States of America. No part of this publication may be reproduced, adapted or transmitted in any form or by any means, electronic or mechanical, including photocopy, recording, or any information storage and retrieval system, without permission in writing from the publisher. For more information, please go to: www.padmorepublishing.com

Cover design: Viveca Batiste
© Cover: Padmore Publishing Group

Library of Congress cataloging in publication data
ISBN: 978-1-939866-08-0 (paperback)

By
Frederick Douglass

Editor's preface

If the volume now presented to the public were a mere work of ART, the history of its misfortune might be written in two very simple words—TOO LATE. The nature and character of slavery have been subjects of an almost endless variety of artistic representation, but this story you are about to read is not a work of ART, but a work of FACTS—Facts, terrible and almost incredible, but yet FACTS, nevertheless.

I am authorized to say that there is not a fictitious name nor place in the whole volume; but that names and places are literally given, and that every transaction therein described actually transpired. Perhaps the best Preface to this book is furnished in the following letter of Mr. Douglass, written in answer to my urgent solicitation for such a work:

ROCHESTER, N. Y. July 2, 1855.

Dear Friend: I have long entertained, as you very well know, a somewhat positive repugnance to writing or speaking anything for the public, which could, with any degree of plausibility, make me liable to the imputation of seeking personal notoriety, for its own sake. Entertaining that feeling very sincerely, and permitting its control, perhaps, quite unreasonably, I have often refused to narrate my personal experience in public anti-slavery meetings, and in sympathizing circles, when urged to do so by friends, with whose views and wishes, ordinarily, it were a pleasure to comply. In my letters and speeches, I have generally aimed to discuss the question of Slavery in the light of fundamental principles, and upon facts, notorious and open to all; making, I trust, no more of the fact of my own former enslavement, than circumstances seemed absolutely to require. I have never placed my opposition to slavery on a basis so narrow as my own enslavement, but rather upon the indestructible and unchangeable laws of human nature, every one of which is perpetually and flagrantly violated by the slave system. I have also felt that it was best for those having histories worth the writing—or supposed to be so—to commit such work to hands other than their own. To write of one's self, in such a manner as not to incur the imputation of weakness, vanity, and egotism, is a work within the ability of but few; and I have little reason to believe that I belong to that fortunate few.

These considerations caused me to hesitate, when first you kindly urged me to prepare for publication a full account of my life as a slave, and my life as a freeman.

Nevertheless, I see, with you, many reasons for regarding my autobiography as exceptional in its character, and as being, in some sense, naturally beyond the reach of those reproaches which honorable and sensitive minds dislike to incur. It is not to illustrate any heroic achievements of a man, but to vindicate a just and beneficent principle, in its application to the whole human family, by letting in the light of truth upon a system, esteemed by some as a blessing, and by others as a curse and a crime. Any facts, either from slaves, slaveholders, or by-standers, calculated to enlighten the public mind, by revealing the true nature, character, and tendency of the slave system, are in order, and can scarcely be innocently withheld.

I see, too, that there are special reasons why I should write my own biography, in preference to employing another to do it. Not only is slavery on trial, but unfortunately, the enslaved people are also on trial. It is alleged, that they are, naturally, inferior; that they are so low in the scale of humanity, and so utterly stupid, that they are unconscious of their wrongs, and do not apprehend their rights. Looking, then, at your request, from this stand-point, and wishing everything of which you think me capable to go to the benefit of my afflicted people, I part with my doubts and hesitation, and proceed to furnish you the desired manuscript; hoping that you may be able to make such arrangements for its publication as shall be best adapted to accomplish that good which you so enthusiastically anticipate.

Frederick Douglass

There was little necessity for doubt and hesitation on the part of Mr. Douglass, as to the propriety of his giving to the world a full account of himself. A man who was born and brought up in slavery, a living witness of its horrors; who often himself experienced its cruelties; and who, despite the depressing influences surrounding his birth, youth and manhood, has risen, from a dark and almost absolute obscurity, to the distinguished position which he now occupies, might very well assume the existence of a commendable curiosity, on the part of the public, to know the facts of his remarkable history.

Editor

1

Childhood

In Talbot county, Eastern Shore, Maryland, near Easton, the county town of that county, there is a small district, thinly populated, and remarkable for nothing that I know of more than for the worn-out, sandy, desert-like appearance of its soil, the general dilapidation of its farms and fences, the indigent and spiritless character of its inhabitants, and the prevalence of ague and fever.

The name of this singularly unpromising and truly famine stricken district is Tuckahoe, a name well known to all Marylanders, black and white. It was given to this section of country probably, at the first, merely in derision; or it may possibly have been applied to it, as I have heard, because someone of its earlier inhabitants had been guilty of the petty meanness of stealing a hoe— or taking a hoe that did not belong to him. Eastern Shore men usually pronounce the word took, as tuck; Took-a-hoe, therefore, is, in Maryland parlance, Tuckahoe.

But, whatever may have been its origin—and about this I will not be positive—that name has stuck to the district in question; and it is seldom mentioned but with contempt, on account of the barrenness of its soil, and the ignorance, and poverty of its people. Decay and ruin are everywhere visible, and the thin population of the place would have quitted it long ago, but for the Choptank river, which runs through it, from which they take abundance of shad and herring, and plenty of ague and fever.

It was in this dull, flat, and unthrifty district, or neighborhood, surrounded by a white population of the lowest order, indolent and drunken to a proverb, and among slaves, who seemed to ask, "Oh! what's the use?" every time they lifted a hoe, that I—without any fault of mine was born, and spent the first years of my childhood.

The reader will pardon so much about the place of my birth, on the score that it is always a fact of some importance to know where a man is born, if, indeed, it be important to know anything about him. In regard to the time of my birth, I cannot be as definite as I have been respecting the place. Nor, indeed, can I impart much knowledge concerning my parents.

Genealogical trees do not flourish among slaves. A person of some consequence here in the north, sometimes designated father, is literally abolished in slave law and slave practice. It is only once in a while that an exception is found to this statement. I never met with a slave who could tell me how old he was. Few slave-mothers know anything of the months of the year, nor of the days of the month. They keep no family records, with marriages, births, and deaths. They measure the ages of their children by spring time, winter time, harvest time, planting time, and the like; but these soon become undistinguishable and forgotten.

Like other slaves, I cannot tell how old I am. This destitution was among my earliest troubles. I learned when I grew up, that my master—and this is the case with masters generally—allowed no questions to be put to him, by which a slave might learn his age. Such questions deemed evidence of impatience, and even of impudent curiosity. From certain events, however, the dates of which I have since learned, I suppose myself to have been born about the year 1817.

The first experience of life that I now remember—and I remember it but hazily—began in the family of my grandmother and grandfather: Betsey and Isaac Baily. They were quite advanced in life, and had long lived on the spot where they then resided. They were considered old settlers in the neighborhood, and, from certain circumstances, I infer that my grandmother, especially, was held in high esteem, far higher than is the lot of most colored persons in the slave states. She was a good nurse, and a capital hand at making nets for catching shad and herring; and these nets were in great demand, not only in Tuckahoe, but at Denton and Hillsboro, neighboring villages. She was not only good at making the nets, but was also somewhat famous for her good fortune in taking the fishes referred to. I have known her to be in the water half the day.

Grandmother was likewise more provident than most of her neighbors in the preservation of seedling sweet potatoes, and it happened to her—as it will happen to any careful and thrifty person residing in an ignorant and improvident community—to enjoy the reputation of having been born to "good luck." Her "good luck" was owing to the exceeding care which she took in preventing the succulent root from getting bruised in the digging, and in placing it beyond the reach of frost, by actually burying it under the hearth of her cabin during the winter months. In the time of planting sweet potatoes, "Grandmother Betty," as she was familiarly called, was sent for in all directions, simply to place the seedling potatoes in the hills; for superstition had it, that if "Grandmamma Betty but touches them at planting, they will be sure to grow and flourish."

This high reputation was full of advantage to her, and to the children around her. Though Tuckahoe had but few of the good things of life, yet of such as it did possess grandmother got a full share, in the way of presents. If good potato crops came after her planting, she was not forgotten by those for whom she planted; and as she was remembered by others, so she remembered the hungry little ones around her.

The dwelling of my grandmother and grandfather had few pretensions. It was a log hut, or cabin, built of clay, wood, and straw. At a distance it resembled—though it was smaller, less commodious and less substantial—the cabins erected in the western states by the first settlers. To my child's eye, however, it was a noble structure, admirably adapted to promote the comforts and conveniences of its inmates. A few rough, Virginia fence rails, flung loosely over the rafters above, answered the triple purpose of floors, ceilings, and bedsteads. To be sure, this upper apartment was reached only by a ladder —but what in the world for climbing could be better than a ladder? To me, this ladder was really a high invention, and possessed a sort of charm as I played with delight upon the rounds of it.

In this little hut there was a large family of children: I dare not say how many. My grandmother—whether because too old for field service, or because she had so faithfully discharged the duties of her station in early life, I know not—enjoyed the high privilege of living in a cabin, separate from the quarter, with no other burden than her own support, and the necessary care of the little children, imposed. She evidently esteemed it a great fortune to live so. The children were not her own, but her grandchildren—the children of her daughters. She took delight in having them around her, and in attending to their few wants.

The practice of separating children from their mothers is a marked feature of the cruelty and barbarity of the slave system. But it is in harmony with the grand aim of slavery to reduce man to a level with the brute. It is a successful method of obliterating from the mind and heart of the slave, all just ideas of the sacredness of the family, as an institution.

Most of the children, however, in this instance, being the children of my grandmother's daughters, the notions of family, and the reciprocal duties and benefits of the relation, had a better chance of being understood than where children are placed—as they often are in the hands of strangers, who have no care for them, apart from the wishes of their masters.

The daughters of my grandmother were five in number. Their names were JENNY, ESTHER, MILLY, PRISCILLA, and HARRIET. The daughter last named was my mother, of whom the reader shall learn more.

Living here, with my dear old grandmother and grandfather, it was a long time before I knew myself to be a slave. I knew many other things before I knew that. Grandmother and grandfather were the greatest people in the world to me; and being with them so snugly in their own little cabin—I supposed it be their own—knowing no higher authority over me or the other children than the authority of grandmamma, for a time there was nothing to disturb me; but, as I grew larger and older, I learned by degrees the sad fact, that the "little hut," and the lot on which it stood, belonged not to my dear old grandparents, but to some person who lived a great distance off, and who was called, by grandmother, "OLD MASTER." I further learned the sadder fact, that not only the house and lot, but that grandmother herself, (grandfather was free,) and all the little children around her, belonged to this mysterious personage, called by grandmother, with every mark of reverence, "Old Master."

Thus early did clouds and shadows begin to fall upon my path. Once on the track—troubles never come singly—I was not long in finding out another fact, still more grievous to my childish heart. I was told that this "old master," whose name seemed ever to be mentioned with fear and shuddering, only allowed the children to live with grandmother for a limited time, and that in fact as soon as they were big enough, they were promptly taken away, to live with the said "old master.".

The absolute power of this distant "old master" had touched my young spirit with but the point of its cold, cruel iron, and left me something to brood over after the play and in moments of repose. Grandmammy was, indeed, at that time, all the world to me; and the thought of being separated from her, in any considerable time, was more than an unwelcome intruder. It was intolerable. Children have their sorrows as well as men and women; SLAVE-children are children, and prove no exceptions to the general rule. The liability to be separated from my grandmother, seldom or never to see her again, haunted me. I dreaded the thought of going to live with that mysterious "old master," whose name I never heard mentioned with affection, but always with fear. I look back to this as among the heaviest of my childhood's sorrows. My grandmother! my grandmother! and the little hut, and the joyous circle under her care, but especially she, who made us sorry when she left us but for an hour, and glad on her return,—how could I leave her and the good old home?

But the sorrows of childhood, like the pleasures of after life, are transient. It is not even within the power of slavery to write indelible sorrow, at a single dash, over the heart of a child.

The tear down childhood's cheek that flows,
Is like the dew-drop on the rose—
When next the summer breeze comes by,
And waves the bush—the flower is dry.

The slaveholder, having nothing to fear from impotent childhood, easily affords to refrain from cruel inflictions; and if cold and hunger do not pierce the tender frame, the first seven or eight years of the slave-boy's life are about as full of sweet content as those of the most favored and petted white children of the slaveholder.

Thus, freed from all restraint, the slave-boy can be a genuine boy, doing whatever his boyish nature suggests. He literally runs wild; has no pretty little verses to learn in the nursery; no nice little speeches to make for aunts, uncles, or cousins, to show how smart he is; and, if he can only manage to keep out of the way of the heavy feet and fists of the older slave boys, he may trot on, in his joyous and roguish tricks, as happy as any little heathen under the palm trees of Africa.

To be sure, he is occasionally reminded, when he stumbles in the path of his master—and this he early learns to avoid—that he is eating his "white bread," and that he will be made to "see sights". The threat is soon forgotten; the shadow soon passes, and our sable boy continues to roll in the dust, or play in the mud, as bests suits him, and in the veriest freedom. If he feels uncomfortable, from mud or from dust, the coast is clear; he can plunge into the river or the pond, without the ceremony of undressing, or the fear of wetting his clothes; his little tow-linen shirt—for that is all he has on—is easily dried; and it needed ablution as much as did his skin.

His food is of the coarsest kind, consisting for the most part of cornmeal mush, which often finds it way from the wooden tray to his mouth in an oyster shell. His days, when the weather is warm, are spent in the pure, open air, and in the bright sunshine. He always sleeps in airy apartments; he seldom has to take powders, or to be paid to swallow pretty little sugar-coated pills, to cleanse his blood, or to quicken his appetite. He eats no candies; gets no lumps of loaf sugar; always relishes his food; cries but little, for nobody cares for his crying; learns to esteem his bruises. In a word, he is, for the most part of the first eight years of his life, a spirited, joyous, uproarious, and happy boy, upon whom troubles fall only like water on a duck's back. And such a boy, so far as I can now remember, was the boy whose life in slavery I am now narrating.

THE SLAVE-BOY ESCAPES MANY TROUBLES WHICH BEFALL AND VEX HIS WHITE BROTHER.

He seldom has to listen to lectures on propriety of behavior, or on anything else.

He is never chided for handling his little knife and fork improperly or awkwardly, for he uses none.

He is never reprimanded for soiling the tablecloth, for he takes his meals on the clay floor.

He never has the misfortune, in his games or sports, of soiling or tearing his clothes, for he has almost none to soil or tear.

He is never expected to act like a nice little gentleman, for he is only a rude little slave.

2

Removed from My First Home

That mysterious individual referred to in the first chapter as an object of terror among the inhabitants of our little cabin, under the ominous title of "old master," was really a man of some consequence. He owned several farms in Tuckahoe; was the chief clerk and butler on the home plantation of Col. Edward Lloyd; had overseers on his own farms; and gave directions to overseers on the farms belonging to Col. Lloyd. This plantation is situated on Wye river—the river receiving its name, doubtless, from Wales, where the Lloyds originated. They (the Lloyds) are an old and honored family in Maryland, exceedingly wealthy. The home plantation, where they have resided, perhaps for a century or more, is one of the largest, most fertile, and best appointed, in the state.

About this plantation, and about that strange old master —who must be something more than a man, and something worse than an angel—the reader will easily imagine that I was not only curious, but eager, to know all that could be known. Unhappily for me, however, all the information I could get concerning him increased my great dread of being separated from and deprived of the protection of my grandmother and grandfather. It was, evidently, a great thing to go to Col. Lloyd's; and I was not without a little curiosity to see the place; but no amount of coaxing could induce in me the wish to remain there.

The fact is, such was my dread of leaving the little cabin, that I wished to remain little forever, for I knew the taller I grew the shorter my stay. The old cabin, with its rail floor and rail bedsteads upstairs, and its clay floor downstairs, and its dirt chimney, and windowless sides, and that most curious piece of workmanship dug in front of the fireplace, beneath which grandmammy placed the sweet potatoes to keep them from the frost, was MY HOME—the only home I ever had; and I loved it, and all connected with it. The old fences around it, and the stumps in the edge of the woods near it, and the squirrels that ran, skipped, and played upon them, were objects of interest and affection. But, in all my sports and plays, and in spite of them, there would, occasionally, come the painful foreboding that I was not long to remain there, and that I must soon be called away to the home of old master.

I was A SLAVE—born a slave and though the fact was incomprehensible to me, it conveyed to my mind a sense of my entire dependence on the will of somebody I had never seen; and, from some cause or other, I had been made to fear this somebody above all else on earth. When the time of my departure was decided upon, my grandmother, knowing my fears, and in pity for them, kindly kept me ignorant of the dreaded event about to transpire. Up to the morning (a beautiful summer morning) when we were to start, and, indeed, during the whole journey—a journey which, child as I was, I remember as well as if it were yesterday—she kept the sad fact hidden from me. This reserve was necessary; for, could I have known all, I should have given grandmother some trouble in getting me started. As it was, I was helpless, and she—dear woman!—led me along by the hand, resisting, with the reserve and solemnity of a priestess, all my inquiring looks to the last.

The distance from Tuckahoe to Wye river—where my old master lived—was full twelve miles, and the walk was quite a severe test of the endurance of my young legs. The journey would have proved too severe for me, but that my dear old grandmother—blessings on her memory!—afforded occasional relief by "toting" me (as Marylanders have it) on her shoulder. My grandmother, though advanced in years—as was evident from more than one gray hair, which peeped from between the ample and graceful folds of her newly-ironed bandana turban—was yet a woman of power and spirit. She was marvelously straight in figure, elastic, and muscular. I seemed hardly to be a burden to her. She would have "toted" me farther, but that I felt myself too much of a man to allow it, and insisted on walking.

Releasing dear grandmamma from carrying me, did not make me altogether independent of her, when we happened to pass through portions of the somber woods which lay between Tuckahoe and Wye river. She often found me increasing the energy of my grip, and holding her clothing, lest something should come out of the woods and eat me up. Several old logs and stumps imposed upon me, and got themselves taken for wild beasts. I could see their legs, eyes, and ears, or I could see something like eyes, legs, and ears, till I got close enough to them to see that the eyes were knots, washed white with rain, and the legs were broken limbs, and the ears, only ears owing to the point from which they were seen. Thus early I learned that the point from which a thing is viewed is of some importance.

As the day advanced the heat increased; and it was not until the afternoon that we reached the much dreaded end of the journey. I found myself in the midst of a group of children of many colors; black, brown, copper colored, and nearly white. I had not seen so many children before. Great houses loomed up in different directions, and a great many men and women were at work in the fields. All this hurry, noise, and singing was very different from the stillness of Tuckahoe. As a new comer, I was an object of special interest; and, after laughing and yelling around me, and playing all sorts of wild tricks, they (the children) asked me to go out and play with them. This I refused to do, preferring to stay with grandmamma. I could not help feeling that our being there boded no good to me. Grandmamma looked sad. She was soon to lose another object of affection, as she had lost many before. I knew she was unhappy, and the shadow fell from her brow on me, though I knew not the cause.

All suspense, however, must have an end; and the end of mine, in this instance, was at hand. Affectionately patting me on the head, and exhorting me to be a good boy, grandmamma told me to go and play with the little children. "They are kin to you," said she; "go and play with them." Among a number of cousins were Phil, Tom, Steve, and Jerry, Nance and Betty.

Grandmother pointed out my brother PERRY, my sister SARAH, and my sister ELIZA, who stood in the group. I had never seen my brother nor my sisters before; and, though I had sometimes heard of them, and felt a curious interest in them, I really did not understand what they were to me, or I to them. We were brothers and sisters, but what of that? Why should they be attached to me, or I to them? Brothers and sisters we were by blood; but slavery had made us strangers. I heard the words brother and sisters, and knew they must mean something; but slavery had robbed these terms of their true meaning. The experience through which I was passing, they had passed through before. They had already been initiated into the mysteries of old master's domicile, and they seemed to look upon me with a certain degree of compassion; but my heart clave to my grandmother. Think it not strange, dear reader, that so little sympathy of feeling existed between us. The conditions of brotherly and sisterly feeling were wanting—we had never nestled and played together. My poor mother, like many other slave-women, had many children, but NO FAMILY! The domestic hearth, with its holy lessons and precious endearments, is abolished in the case of a slave-mother and her children. "Little children, love one another," are words seldom heard in a slave cabin.

I really wanted to play with my brother and sisters, but they were strangers to me, and I was full of fear that grandmother might leave without taking me with her. Entreated to do so, however, and that, too, by my dear grandmother, I went to the back part of the house, to play with them and the other children. Play, however, I did not, but stood with my back against the wall, witnessing the playing of the others. At last, while standing there, one of the children, who had been in the kitchen, ran up to me, in a sort of roguish glee, exclaiming, "Fed, Fed! grandmammy gone! grandmammy gone!"

I could not believe it; yet, fearing the worst, I ran into the kitchen, to see for myself, and found it even so. Grandmammy had indeed gone, and was now far away, "clean" out of sight. I need not tell all that happened now. Almost heartbroken at the discovery, I fell upon the ground, and wept a boy's bitter tears, refusing to be comforted. My brother and sisters came around me, and said, "Don't cry," and gave me peaches and pears, but I flung them away, and refused all their kindly advances. I had never been deceived before; and I felt not only grieved at parting—as I supposed forever—with my grandmother, but indignant that a trick had been played upon me in a matter so serious.

It was now late in the afternoon. The day had been an exciting and wearisome one, and I knew not how or where, but I suppose I sobbed myself to sleep. There is a healing in the angel wing of sleep, even for the slave-boy; and its balm was never more welcome to any wounded soul than it was to mine, the first night I spent at the domicile of old master. The reader may be surprised that I narrate so minutely an incident apparently so trivial, and which must have occurred when I was not more than seven years old; but as I wish to give a faithful history of my experience in slavery, I cannot withhold a circumstance which, at the time, affected me so deeply. Besides, this was, in fact, my first introduction to the realities of slavery.

3

Parentage

If the reader will now be kind enough to allow me time to grow bigger, and afford me an opportunity for my experience to become greater, I will tell him something, by-and-by, of slave life, as I saw, felt, and heard it, on Col. Edward Lloyd's plantation, and at the house of old master, where I had now, despite of myself, most suddenly, but not unexpectedly, been dropped. Meanwhile, I will redeem my promise to say something more of my dear mother.

I say nothing of father, for he is shrouded in a mystery I have never been able to penetrate. Slavery does away with fathers, as it does away with families. Slavery has no use for either fathers or families, and its laws do not recognize their existence in the social arrangements of the plantation. When they do exist, they are not the outgrowths of slavery, but are antagonistic to that system. The order of civilization is reversed here. The name of the child is not expected to be that of its father, and his condition does not necessarily affect that of the child. He may be the slave of Mr. Tilgman; and his child, when born, may be the slave of Mr. Gross. He may be a freeman; and yet his child may be a chattel. He may be white, glorying in the purity of his Anglo-Saxon blood; and his child may be ranked with the blackest slaves. Indeed, he may be, and often is, master and father to the same child. He can be father without being a husband, and may sell his child without incurring reproach, if the child be by a woman in whose veins courses one thirty-second part of African blood.

But to return, or rather, to begin. My knowledge of my mother is very scanty, but very distinct. Her personal appearance and bearing are ineffaceably stamped upon my memory. She was tall, and finely proportioned; of deep black, glossy complexion; had regular features, and, among the other slaves, was remarkably sedate in her manners. There is in Prichard's Natural History of Man, the head of a figure—on page 157—the features of which so resemble those of my mother, that I often recur to it with something of the feeling which I suppose others experience when looking upon the pictures of dear departed ones.

Yet I cannot say that I was very deeply attached to my mother; certainly not so deeply as I should have been had our relations in childhood been different. We were separated, according to the common custom, when I was but an infant, and, of course, before I knew my mother from anyone else. The slave-mother can be spared long enough from the field to endure all the bitterness of a mother's anguish, when it adds another name to a master's ledger, but not long enough to receive the joyous reward afforded by the intelligent smiles of her child. I never think of this terrible interference of slavery with my infantile affections, and its diverting them from their natural course, without feelings to which I can give no adequate expression.

I do not remember to have seen my mother at my grandmother's at any time. I remember her only in her visits to me at Col. Lloyd's plantation, and in the kitchen of my old master. Her visits to me there were few in number, brief in duration, and mostly made in the night. The pains she took, and the toil she endured, to see me, tells me that a true mother's heart was hers, and that slavery had difficulty in paralyzing it with unmotherly indifference.

My mother was hired out to a Mr. Stewart, who lived about twelve miles from old master's, and, being a field hand, she seldom had leisure, by day, for the performance of the journey. The nights and the distance were both obstacles to her visits. She was obliged to walk, unless chance flung into her way an opportunity to ride; and the latter was sometimes her good luck. But she always had to walk one way or the other. It was a greater luxury than slavery could afford, to allow a black slave- mother a horse or a mule, upon which to travel twenty-four miles, when she could walk the distance. Besides, it is deemed a foolish whim for a slave-mother to manifest concern to see her children, and, in one point of view, the case is made out—she can do nothing for them. She has no control over them; the master is even more than the mother, in all matters touching the fate of her child. Why, then, should she give herself any concern? She has no responsibility. Such is the reasoning, and such the practice. The iron rule of the plantation, always passionately and violently enforced in that neighborhood, makes flogging the penalty of failing to be in the field before sunrise in the morning, unless special permission be given to the absenting slave. "I went to see my child," is no excuse to the ear or heart of the overseer.

One of the visits of my mother to me, while at Col. Lloyd's, I remember very vividly, as affording a bright gleam of a mother's love, and the earnestness of a mother's care.

"I had on that day offended "Aunt Katy," (called "Aunt" by way of respect,) the cook of old master's establishment. I do not now remember the nature of my offense in this instance, for my offenses were numerous in that quarter, greatly depending, however, upon the mood of Aunt Katy, as to their heinousness; but she had adopted, that day, her favorite mode of punishing me, namely, making me go without food all day—that is, from after breakfast. The first hour or two after dinner, I succeeded pretty well in keeping up my spirits; but though I made an excellent stand against the foe, and fought bravely during the afternoon, I knew I must be conquered at last, unless I got the accustomed reenforcement of a slice of corn bread, at sundown. Sundown came, but no bread, and, in its stead, their came the threat, with a scowl well suited to its terrible import, that she "meant to starve the life out of me!" Brandishing her knife, she chopped off the heavy slices for the other children, and put the loaf away, muttering, all the while, her savage designs upon myself. Against this disappointment, for I was expecting that her heart would relent at last, I made an extra effort to maintain my dignity; but when I saw all the other children around me with merry and satisfied faces, I could stand it no longer. I went out behind the house, and cried like a fine fellow!

When tired of this, I returned to the kitchen, sat by the fire, and brooded over my hard lot. I was too hungry to sleep. While I sat in the corner, I caught sight of an ear of Indian corn on an upper shelf of the kitchen. I watched my chance, and got it, and, shelling off a few grains, I put it back again. The grains in my hand, I quickly put in some ashes, and covered them with embers, to roast them. All this I did at the risk of getting a brutal thumping, for Aunt Katy could beat, as well as starve me. My corn was not long in roasting, and, with my keen appetite, it did not matter even if the grains were not exactly done. I eagerly pulled them out, and placed them on my stool, in a clever little pile. Just as I began to help myself to my very dry meal, in came my dear mother. And now, dear reader, a scene occurred which was altogether worth beholding, and to me it was instructive as well as interesting.

The friendless and hungry boy, in his extremest need—and when he did not dare to look for succor—found himself in the strong, protecting arms of a mother; a mother who was, at the moment (being endowed with high powers of manner as well as matter) more than a match for all his enemies. I shall never forget the indescribable expression of her countenance, when I told her that I had had no food since morning; and that Aunt Katy said she "meant to starve the life out of me." There was pity in her glance at me, and a fiery indignation at Aunt Katy at the same time; and, while she took the corn from me, and gave me a large ginger cake, in its stead, she read Aunt Katy a lecture which she never forgot.

My mother threatened her with complaining to old master in my behalf; for the latter, though harsh and cruel himself, at times, did not sanction the meanness, injustice, partiality and oppressions enacted by Aunt Katy in the kitchen. That night I learned the fact, that I was, not only a child, but somebody's child. The "sweet cake" my mother gave me was in the shape of a heart, with a rich, dark ring glazed upon the edge of it. I was victorious, and well off for the moment; prouder, on my mother's knee, than a king upon his throne. But my triumph was short. I dropped off to sleep, and waked in the morning only to find my mother gone, and myself left at the mercy of the sable virago, dominant in my old master's kitchen, whose fiery wrath was my constant dread.

I do not remember to have seen my mother after this occurrence. Death soon ended the little communication that had existed between us; and with it, I believe, a life judging from her weary, sad, downcast countenance and mute demeanor—full of heartfelt sorrow. I was not allowed to visit her during any part of her long illness; nor did I see her for a long time before she was taken ill and died. The heartless and ghastly form of slavery rises between mother and child, even at the bed of death. The mother, at the verge of the grave, may not gather her children, to impart to them her holy admonitions, and invoke for them her dying benediction. The bond-woman lives as a slave, and is left to die as a beast; often with fewer attentions than are paid to a favorite horse. Scenes of sacred tenderness, around the death-bed, never forgotten, and which often arrest the vicious and confirm the virtuous during life, must be looked for among the free, though they sometimes occur among the slaves. It has been a life-long, standing grief to me, that I knew so little of my mother; and that I was so early separated from her. The counsels of her love must have been beneficial to me. The side view of her face is imaged on my memory, and I take few steps in life, without feeling her presence; but the image is mute, and I have no striking words of her's treasured up.

I learned, after my mother's death, that she could read, and that she was the only one of all the slaves and colored people in Tuckahoe who enjoyed that advantage. How she acquired this knowledge, I know not, for Tuckahoe is the last place in the world where she would be apt to find facilities for learning. I can, therefore, fondly and proudly ascribe to her an earnest love of knowledge. That a "field hand" should learn to read, in any slave state, is remarkable; but the achievement of my mother, considering the place, was very extraordinary; and, in view of that fact, I am quite willing, and even happy, to attribute any love of letters I possess, and for which I have got—despite of prejudices only too much credit, not to my admitted Anglo-Saxon paternity, but to the native genius of my unprotected, and uncultivated mother—a woman, who belonged to a race whose mental endowments it is, at present, fashionable to hold in disparagement and contempt.

Summoned away to her account, with the impassable gulf of slavery between us during her entire illness, my mother died without leaving me a single intimation of who my father was. There was a whisper, that my master was my father; yet it was only a whisper, and I cannot say that I ever gave it credence. Indeed, I now have reason to think he was not; nevertheless, the fact remains, in all its glaring odiousness, that, by the laws of slavery, children, in all cases, are reduced to the condition of their mothers. This arrangement admits of the greatest license to brutal slaveholders, and their profligate sons, brothers, relations and friends, and gives to the pleasure of sin, the additional attraction of profit. A whole volume might be written on this single feature of slavery, as I have observed it.

One might imagine, that the children of such connections, would fare better, in the hands of their masters, than other slaves. The rule is quite the other way; and a very little reflection will satisfy the reader that such is the case. A man who will enslave his own blood, may not be safely relied on for magnanimity. Men do not love those who remind them of their sins unless they have a mind to repent—and the mulatto child's face is a standing accusation against him who is master and father to the child.

What is still worse, perhaps, such a child is a constant offense to the wife. She hates its very presence, and when a slaveholding woman hates, she wants not means to give that hate telling effect. Women—white women, I mean— are IDOLS at the south, not WIVES, for the slave women are preferred in many instances; and if these idols but nod, or lift a finger, woe to the poor victim: kicks, cuffs and stripes are sure to follow. Masters are frequently compelled to sell this class of their slaves, out of deference to the feelings of their white wives; and shocking and scandalous as it may seem for a man to sell his own blood to the traffickers in human flesh, it is often an act of humanity toward the slave-child to be thus removed from his merciless tormentors.

After what I have now said of the circumstances of my mother, and my relations to her, the reader will not be surprised, nor be disposed to censure me, when I tell but the simple truth, viz: that I received the tidings of her death with no strong emotions of sorrow for her, and with very little regret for myself on account of her loss. I had to learn the value of my mother long after her death, and by witnessing the devotion of other mothers to their children.

There is not, beneath the sky, an enemy to filial affection so destructive as slavery. It had made my brothers and sisters strangers to me; it converted the mother that bore me, into a myth; it shrouded my father in mystery, and left me without an intelligible beginning in the world.

My mother died when I could not have been more than eight or nine years old, on one of old master's farms in Tuckahoe, in the neighborhood of Hillsborough. Her grave is, as the grave of the dead at sea, unmarked, and without stone or stake.

4

The Plantation

It is generally supposed that slavery, in the state of Maryland, exists in its mildest form, and that it is totally divested of those harsh and terrible peculiarities, which mark and characterize the slave system, in the southern and south-western states of the American union. The argument in favor of this opinion, is the contiguity of the free states, and the exposed condition of slavery in Maryland to the moral, religious and humane sentiment of the free states.

I am not about to refute this argument, so far as it relates to slavery in that state, generally; on the contrary, I am willing to admit that, to this general point, the arguments is well grounded. Public opinion is, indeed, an unfailing restraint upon the cruelty and barbarity of masters, overseers, and slave-drivers, whenever and wherever it can reach them; but there are certain secluded and out-of-the-way places, even in the state of Maryland, seldom visited by a single ray of healthy public sentiment—where slavery, wrapt in its own congenial, mid-night darkness, can, and does, develop all its malign and shocking characteristics; where it can be indecent without shame, cruel without shuddering, and murderous without apprehension or fear of exposure.

Just such a secluded, dark, and out-of-the-way place, is the "home plantation" of Col. Edward Lloyd, on the Eastern Shore, Maryland. It is far away from all the great thoroughfares, and is proximate to no town or village. There is neither school-house, nor town-house in its neighborhood. The school-house is unnecessary, for there are no children to go to school.

The children and grandchildren of Col. Lloyd were taught in the house, by a private tutor—Mr. Page, a tall, gaunt sapling of a man, who did not speak a dozen words to a slave in a whole year. The overseers' children go off somewhere to school; and they, therefore, bring no foreign or dangerous influence from abroad, to embarrass the natural operation of the slave system of the place. Its whole public is made up of, and divided into, three classes—SLAVEHOLDERS, SLAVES and OVERSEERS. Its blacksmiths, wheelwrights, shoemakers, weavers, and coopers, are slaves.

Whether with a view of guarding against the escape of its secrets, I know not, but it is a fact, the every leaf and grain of the produce of this plantation, and those of the neighboring farms belonging to Col. Lloyd, are transported to Baltimore in Col. Lloyd's own vessels; every man and boy on board of which—except the captain—are owned by him. In return, everything brought to the plantation, comes through the same channel. Thus, even the glimmering and unsteady light of trade, which sometimes exerts a civilizing influence, is excluded from this "tabooed" spot.

Nearly all the plantations or farms in the vicinity of the "home plantation" of Col. Lloyd, belong to him; and those which do not, are owned by personal friends of his, as deeply interested in maintaining the slave system, in all its rigor, as Col. Lloyd himself. Some of his neighbors are said to be even more stringent than he. The Skinners, the Peakers, the Tilgmans, the Lockermans, and the Gipsons, are in the same boat; being slaveholding neighbors, they may have strengthened each other in their iron rule. They are on intimate terms, and their interests and tastes are identical.

Col. Lloyd's plantation is a little nation of its own, having its own language, its own rules, regulations and customs. The laws and institutions of the state, apparently touch it nowhere. The troubles arising here, are not settled by the civil power of the state. The overseer is generally accuser, judge, jury, advocate and executioner. The criminal is always dumb. The overseer attends to all sides of a case.

In its isolation, seclusion, and self-reliant independence, Col. Lloyd's plantation resembles what the baronial domains were during the middle ages in Europe. Grim, cold, and unapproachable by all genial influences from communities without, there it stands; full three hundred years behind the age, in all that relates to humanity and morals.

This, however, is not the only view that the place presents. Civilization is shut out, but nature cannot be. Though separated from the rest of the world; though public opinion, as I have said, seldom gets a chance to penetrate its dark domain; though the whole place is stamped with its own peculiar, iron- like individuality; and though crimes, high-handed and atrocious, may there be committed, with almost as much impunity as upon the deck of a pirate ship—it is, nevertheless, altogether, to outward seeming, a most strikingly interesting place, full of life, activity, and spirit; and presents a very favorable contrast to the indolent monotony and languor of Tuckahoe.

Keen as was my regret and great as was my sorrow at leaving the latter, I was not long in adapting myself to this, my new home. A man's troubles are always half disposed of, when he finds endurance his only remedy. I found myself here; there was no getting away; and what remained for me, but to make the best of it? Here were plenty of children to play with, and plenty of places of pleasant resort for boys of my age, and boys older. The little tendrils of affection, so rudely and treacherously broken from around the darling objects of my grandmother's hut, gradually began to extend, and to entwine about the new objects by which I now found myself surrounded.

There was a windmill (always a commanding object to a child's eye) on Long Point—a tract of land dividing Miles river from the Wye a mile or more from my old master's house. There was a creek to swim in, at the bottom of an open flat space, of twenty acres or more, called "the Long Green"—a very beautiful playground for the children.

In the river, a short distance from the shore, lying quietly at anchor, with her small boat dancing at her stern, was a large sloop—the Sally Lloyd; called by that name in honor of a favorite daughter of the colonel. The sloop and the mill were wondrous things, full of thoughts and ideas. A child cannot well look at such objects without thinking.

Then here were a great many houses; human habitations, full of the mysteries of life at every stage of it. There was the little red house, up the road, occupied by Mr. Sevier, the overseer. A little nearer to my old master's, stood a very long, rough, low building, literally alive with slaves, of all ages, conditions and sizes. This was called "the Longe Quarter." Perched upon a hill, across the Long Green, was a very tall, dilapidated, old brick building—the architectural dimensions of which proclaimed its erection for a different purpose—now occupied by slaves, in a similar manner to the Long Quarter. Besides these, there were numerous other slave houses and huts, scattered around in the neighborhood, every nook and corner of which was completely occupied. Old master's house, a long, brick building, plain, but substantial, stood in the center of the plantation life, and constituted one independent establishment on the premises of Col. Lloyd. Besides these dwellings, there were barns, stables, storehouses, and tobacco-houses; blacksmiths' shops, wheelwrights' shops, coopers' shops—all objects of interest; but, above all, there stood the grandest building my eyes had then ever beheld, called, by every one on the plantation, the "Great House." This was occupied by Col. Lloyd and his family. They occupied it; I enjoyed it. The great house was surrounded by numerous and variously shaped out-buildings. There were kitchens, wash- houses, dairies, summer-house, green-houses, hen-houses, turkey-houses, pigeon-houses, and arbors, of many sizes and devices, all neatly painted, and altogether interspersed with grand old trees, ornamental and primitive, which afforded delightful shade in summer, and imparted to the scene a high degree of stately beauty. The great house itself was a large, white, wooden building, with wings on three sides of it. In front, a large portico, extending the entire length of the building, and supported by a long range of columns, gave to the whole establishment an air of solemn grandeur.

It was a treat to my young and gradually opening mind, to behold this elaborate exhibition of wealth, power, and vanity. The carriage entrance to the house was a large gate, more than a quarter of a mile distant from it; the intermediate space was a beautiful lawn, very neatly trimmed, and watched with the greatest care. It was dotted thickly over with delightful trees, shrubbery, and flowers. The road, or lane, from the gate to the great house, was richly paved with white pebbles from the beach, and, in its course, formed a complete circle around the beautiful lawn. Carriages going in and retiring from the great house, made the circuit of the lawn, and their passengers were permitted to behold a scene of almost Eden-like beauty. Outside this select inclosure, were parks, where as about the residences of the English nobility—rabbits, deer, and other wild game, might be seen, peering and playing about, with none to molest them or make them afraid. The tops of the stately poplars were often covered with the red-winged black-birds, making all nature vocal with the joyous life and beauty of their wild, warbling notes. These all belonged to me, as well as to Col. Edward Lloyd, and for a time I greatly enjoyed them.

A short distance from the great house, were the stately mansions of the dead, a place of somber aspect. Vast tombs, embowered beneath the weeping willow and the fir tree, told of the antiquities of the Lloyd family, as well as of their wealth. Superstition was rife among the slaves about this family bury- ing ground. Strange sights had been seen there by some of the older slaves. Shrouded ghosts, riding on great black horses, had been seen to enter; balls of fire had been seen to fly there at midnight, and horrid sounds had been repeatedly heard. Slaves know enough of the rudiments of theology to believe that those go to hell who die slaveholders; and they often fancy such persons wishing themselves back again, to wield the lash. Tales of sights and sounds, strange and terrible, connected with the huge black tombs, were a very great security to the grounds about them, for few of the slaves felt like approaching them even in the day time. It was a dark, gloomy and forbidding place, and it was difficult to feel that the spirits of the sleeping dust there deposited, reigned with the blest in the realms of eternal peace.

The business of twenty or thirty farms was transacted at this, called, by way of eminence, "great house farm." These farms all belonged to Col. Lloyd, as did, also, the slaves upon them. Each farm was under the management of an overseer. As I have said of the overseer of the home plantation, so I may say of the overseers on the smaller ones; they stand between the slave and all civil constitutions—their word is law, and is implicitly obeyed.

THE LAWS OF THE PLANTATION:

*-There are no conflicting rights of property,
for all the people are owned by one man;
and they can themselves own no property.*

-Religion and politics are alike excluded.

*-One class of the population is too high
to be reached by the preacher;
and the other class is too low
to be cared for by the preacher.*

*-The poor have the gospel preached to them,
in this neighborhood, only when
they are able to pay for it.
The slaves, having no money, get no gospel.*

*-The politician keeps away, because the people
have no votes, and the preacher keeps away,
because the people have no money.*

*-The rich planter can afford to learn politics
in the parlor, and to dispense
with religion altogether.*

The colonel, at this time, was reputed to be, and he apparently was, very rich. His slaves, alone, were an immense fortune. These, small and great, could not have been fewer than one thousand in number, and though scarcely a month passed without the sale of one or more lots to the Georgia traders, there was no apparent diminution in the number of his human stock: the home plantation merely groaned at a removal of the young increase, or human crop, then proceeded as lively as ever.

Horse-shoeing, cart-mending, plow-repairing, coopering, grinding, and weaving, for all the neighboring farms, were performed here, and slaves were employed in all these branches. "Uncle Tony" was the blacksmith; "Uncle Harry" was the cartwright; "Uncle Abel" was the shoemaker; and all these had hands to assist them in their several departments.

These mechanics were called "uncles" by all the younger slaves, not because they really sustained that relationship to any, but according to plantation etiquette, as a mark of respect, due from the younger to the older slaves. Strange, and even ridiculous as it may seem, among a people so uncultivated, and with so many stern trials to look in the face, there is not to be found, among any people, a more rigid enforcement of the law of respect to elders, than they maintain. I set this down as partly constitutional with my race, and partly conventional. There is no better material in the world for making a gentleman, than is furnished in the African. He shows to others, and exacts for himself, all the tokens of respect which he is compelled to manifest toward his master. A young slave must approach the company of the older with hat in hand, and woe betide him, if he fails to acknowledge a favor, of any sort, with the accustomed "tank'ee," etc. So uniformly are good manners enforced among slaves, I can easily detect a "bogus" fugitive by his manners.

Among other slave notabilities of the plantation, was one called by everybody Uncle Isaac Copper. It is seldom that a slave gets a surname from anybody in Maryland; and so completely has the south shaped the manners of the north, in this respect, that even abolitionists make very little of the surname of a Negro. The only improvement on the "Bills," "Jacks," "Jims," and "Neds" of the south, observable here is, that "William," "John," "James," "Edward," are substituted. It goes against the grain to treat and address a Negro precisely as they would treat and address a white man. But, once in a while, in slavery as in the free states, by some extraordinary circumstance, the Negro has a surname fastened to him, and holds it against all conventionalities.

This was the case with Uncle Isaac Copper. When the "uncle" was dropped, he generally had the prefix "doctor," in its stead. He was our doctor of medicine, and doctor of divinity as well. Where he took his degree I am unable to say, for he was not very communicative to inferiors, and I was emphatically such, being but a boy seven or eight years old. He was too well established in his profession to permit questions as to his native skill, or his attainments. One qualification he undoubtedly had—he was a confirmed cripple; and he could neither work, nor would he bring anything if offered for sale in the market. The old man, though lame, was no sluggard. He was a man that made his crutches do him good service. He was always on the alert, looking up the sick, and all such as were supposed to need his counsel. His remedial prescriptions embraced four articles. For diseases of the body, Epsom salts and castor oil; for those of the soul, the Lord's Prayer, and hickory switches!

I was not long at Col. Lloyd's before I was placed under the care of Doctor Issac Copper. I was sent to him with twenty or thirty other children, to learn the "Lord's Prayer." I found the old gentleman seated on a huge three-legged oaken stool, armed with several large hickory switches; and, from his position, he could reach —lame as he was—any boy in the room. After standing awhile to learn what was expected of us, the old gentleman, in any other than a devotional tone, commanded us to kneel down. This done, he commenced telling us to say everything he said. "Our Father"—this was repeated after him with promptness and uniformity; "Who art in heaven"—was less promptly and uniformly repeated; and the old gentleman paused in the prayer, to give us a short lecture upon the consequences of inattention, both immediate and future, and especially those more immediate. About these he was absolutely certain, for he held in his right hand the means of bringing all his predictions and warnings to pass. On he proceeded with the prayer; and we with our thick tongues and unskilled ears, followed him to the best of our ability. This, however, was not sufficient to please the old gentleman. Everybody, in the south, wants the privilege of whipping somebody else. Uncle Isaac shared the common passion of his country, and, therefore, seldom found any means of keeping his disciples in order short of flogging.

"Say everything I say;" and bang would come the switch on some poor boy's undevotional head. "What you looking at there"—"Stop that pushing"—and down again would come the lash.

The whip is all in all. It is supposed to secure obedience to the slaveholder, and is held as a sovereign remedy among the slaves themselves, for every form of disobedience, temporal or spiritual. Slaves, as well as slaveholders, use it with an unsparing hand. Our devotions at Uncle Isaac's combined too much of the tragic and comic, to make them very salutary in a spiritual point of view; and it is due to truth to say, I was often a truant when the time for attending the praying and flogging of Doctor Isaac Copper came on.

The windmill under the care of Mr. Kinney, a kind hearted old Englishman, was to me a source of infinite interest and pleasure. The old man always seemed pleased when he saw a troop of darkey little urchins, with their tow-linen shirts fluttering in the breeze, approaching to view and admire the whirling wings of his wondrous machine. From the mill we could see other objects of deep interest. These were, the vessels from St. Michael's, on their way to Baltimore. It was a source of much amusement to view the flowing sails and complicated rigging, as the little crafts dashed by, and to speculate upon Baltimore, as to the kind and quality of the place.

With so many sources of interest around me, the reader may be prepared to learn that I began to think very highly of Col. L.'s plantation. It was just a place to my boyish taste. There were fish to be caught in the creek, if one only had a hook and line; and crabs, clams and oysters were to be caught by wading, digging and raking for them. Here was a field for industry and enterprise, strongly inviting; and the reader may be assured that I entered upon it with spirit.

Even the much dreaded old master, whose merciless fiat had brought me from Tuckahoe, gradually, to my mind, parted with his terrors. Strange enough, his reverence seemed to take no particular notice of me, nor of my coming. Instead of leaping out and devouring me, he scarcely seemed conscious of my presence. The fact is, he was occupied with matters more weighty and important than either looking after or vexing me. He probably thought as little of my advent, as he would have thought of the addition of a single pig to his stock!

As the chief butler on Col. Lloyd's plantation, his duties were numerous and perplexing. In almost all important matters he answered in Col. Lloyd's stead. The overseers of all the farms were in some sort under him, and received the law from his mouth. The colonel himself seldom addressed an overseer, or allowed an overseer to address him. Old master carried the keys of all store houses; measured out the allowance for each slave at the end of every month; superintended the storing of all goods brought to the plantation; dealt out the raw material to all the handicraftsmen; shipped the grain, tobacco, and all saleable produce of the plantation to market, and had the general oversight of the coopers' shop, wheelwrights' shop, blacksmiths' shop, and shoemakers' shop. Besides the care of these, he often had business for the plantation which required him to be absent two and three days.

Thus largely employed, he had little time, and perhaps as little disposition, to interfere with the children individually. What he was to Col. Lloyd, he made Aunt Katy to him. When he had anything to say or do about us, it was said or done in a wholesale manner; disposing of us in classes or sizes, leaving all minor details to Aunt

Katy, a person of whom the reader has already received no very favorable impression. Aunt Katy was a woman who never allowed herself to act greatly within the margin of power granted to her, no matter how broad that authority might be. Ambitious, ill-tempered and cruel, she found in her present position an ample field for the exercise of her ill- omened qualities. She had a strong hold on old master, she was considered a first rate cook, and she really was very industrious. She was, therefore, greatly favored by old master, and as one mark of his favor, she was the only mother who was permitted to retain her children around her.

Even to these children she was often fiendish in her brutality. She pursued her son Phil, one day, in my presence, with a huge butcher knife, and dealt a blow with its edge which left a shocking gash on his arm, near the wrist. For this, old master did sharply rebuke her, and threatened that if she ever should do the like again, he would take the skin off her back. Cruel, however, as Aunt Katy was to her own children, at times she was not destitute of maternal feeling, as I often had occasion to know, in the bitter pinches of hunger I had to endure. Differing from the practice of Col. Lloyd, old master, instead of allowing so much for each slave, committed the allowance for all to the care of Aunt Katy, to be divided after cooking it, amongst us. The allowance, consisting of coarse cornmeal, was not very abundant—indeed, it was very slender; and in passing through Aunt Katy's hands, it was made more slender still, for some of us. William, Phil and Jerry were her children, and it is not to accuse her too severely, to allege that she was often guilty of starving myself and the other children, while she was literally cramming her own.

Want of food was my chief trouble the first summer at my old master's. Oysters and clams would do very well, with an occasional supply of bread, but they soon failed in the absence of bread. I speak but the simple truth, when I say, I have often been so pinched with hunger, that I have fought with the dog—"Old Nep"—for the smallest crumbs that fell from the kitchen table, and have been glad when I won a single crumb in the combat. Many times have I followed, with eager step, the waiting-girl when she went out to shake the table cloth, to get the crumbs and small bones flung out for the cats. The water, in which meat had been boiled, was as eagerly sought for by me. It was a great thing to get the privilege of dipping a piece of bread in such water; and the skin taken from rusty bacon, was a positive luxury. Nevertheless, I sometimes got full meals and kind words from sympathizing old slaves, who knew my sufferings, and received the comforting assurance that I should be a man some day.

"Never mind, honey—better day comin'," was even then a solace, a cheering consolation to me in my troubles. Nor were all the kind words I received from slaves. I had a friend in the parlor, as well, and one to whom I shall be glad to do justice, before I have finished this part of my story.

I was not long at old master's, before I learned that his surname was Anthony, and that he was generally called "Captain Anthony"—a title which he probably acquired by sailing a craft in the Chesapeake Bay. Col. Lloyd's slaves never called Capt. Anthony "old master," but always Capt. Anthony; and me they called "Captain Anthony Fred." There is not, probably, in the whole south, a plantation where the English language is more imperfectly spoken than on Col. Lloyd's. It is a mixture of Guinea and everything else you please. At the time of which I am now writing, there were slaves there who had been brought from the coast of Africa. They never used the "s" in indication of the possessive case. "Cap'n Ant'ney Tom," "Lloyd Bill," "Aunt Rose Harry," means "Captain Anthony's Tom," "Lloyd's Bill," etc. "Oo you dem long to?" means, "Whom do you belong to?" "Oo dem got any peachy?" means, "Have you got any peaches?" I could scarcely understand them when I first went among them, so broken was their speech; and I am persuaded that I could not have been dropped anywhere on the globe, where I could reap less, in the way of knowledge, from my immediate associates, than on this plantation. Even "MAS' DANIEL," by his association with his father's slaves, had measurably adopted their dialect and their ideas, so far as they had ideas to be adopted.

The equality of nature is strongly asserted in childhood, and childhood requires children for associates. Color makes no difference with a child. Are you a child with wants, tastes and pursuits common to children, not put on, but natural? then, were you black as ebony you would be welcome to the child of alabaster whiteness. The law of compensation holds here, as well as elsewhere. Mas' Daniel could not associate with ignorance without sharing its shade; and he could not give his black playmates his company, without giving them his intelligence, as well. Without knowing this, or caring about it, at the time, I, for some cause or other, spent much of my time with Mas' Daniel, in preference to spending it with most of the other boys.

Mas' Daniel was the youngest son of Col. Lloyd; his older brothers were Edward and Murray—both grown up, and fine looking men. Edward was especially esteemed by the children, and by me among the rest; not that he ever said anything to us or for us, which could be called especially kind; it was enough for us, that he never looked nor acted scornfully toward us. There were also three sisters, all married; one to Edward Winder; a second to Edward Nicholson; a third to Mr. Lownes.

The family of old master consisted of two sons, Andrew and Richard; his daughter, Lucretia, and her newly married husband, Capt. Auld. This was the house family. The kitchen family consisted of Aunt Katy, Aunt Esther, and ten or a dozen children, most of them older than myself. Capt. Anthony was not considered a rich slaveholder, but was pretty well off in the world. He owned about thirty "head" of slaves, and three farms in Tuckahoe. The most valuable part of his property was his slaves, of whom he could afford to sell one every year. This crop, therefore, brought him seven or eight hundred dollars a year, besides his yearly salary, and other revenue from his farms.

The idea of rank and station was rigidly maintained on Col. Lloyd's plantation. Our family never visited the great house, and the Lloyds never came to our home. Equal non-intercourse was observed between Capt. Anthony's family and that of Mr. Sevier, the overseer.

Such, kind reader, was the community, and such the place, in which my earliest and most lasting impressions of slavery, and of slave-life, were received; of which impressions you will learn more in the coming chapters of this book.

5

Initiation to the Mysteries of Slavery

Although my old master—Capt. Anthony—gave me at first, (as the reader will have already seen) very little attention, and although that little was of a remarkably mild and gentle description, a few months only were sufficient to convince me that mildness and gentleness were not the prevailing or governing traits of his character. These excellent qualities were displayed only occasionally. He could, when it suited him, appear to be literally insensible to the claims of humanity, when appealed to by the helpless against an aggressor, and he could himself commit outrages, deep, dark and nameless. Yet he was not by nature worse than other men. Had he been brought up in a free state, surrounded by the just restraints of free society—restraints which are necessary to the freedom of all its members, alike and equally—Capt. Anthony might have been as humane a man, and every way as respectable, as many who now oppose the slave system; certainly as humane and respectable as are members of society generally. The slave-holder, as well as the slave, is the victim of the slave system. A man's character greatly takes its hue and shape from the form and color of things about him. Under the whole heavens there is no relation more unfavorable to the development of honorable character, than that sustained by the slaveholder to the slave.

Reason is imprisoned here, and passions run wild. Like the fires of the prairie, once lighted, they are at the mercy of every wind, and must burn, till they have consumed all that is combustible within their remorseless grasp. Capt. Anthony could be kind, and, at times, he even showed an affectionate disposition. Could the reader have seen him gently leading me by the hand—as he sometimes did—patting me on the head, speaking to me in soft, caressing tones and calling me his "little Indian boy," he would have deemed him a kind old man, and really, almost fatherly. But the pleasant moods of a slave-holder are remarkably brittle; they are easily snapped; they neither come often, nor remain long. His temper is subjected to perpetual trials; but, since these trials are never borne patiently, they add nothing to his natural stock of patience.

Old master very early impressed me with the idea that he was an unhappy man. Even to my child's eye, he wore a troubled, and at times, a haggard aspect. His strange movements excited my curiosity, and awakened my compassion. He seldom walked alone without muttering to himself; and he occasionally stormed about, as if defying an army of invisible foes. "He would do this, that, and the other; he'd be d—d if he did not,"—was the usual form of his threats. Most of his leisure was spent in walking, cursing and gesticulating, like one possessed by a demon. Most evidently, he was a wretched man, at war with his own soul, and with all the world around him.

To be overheard by the children, disturbed him very little. He made no more of our presence, than of that of the ducks and geese which he met on the green. He little thought that the little black urchins around him, could see, through those vocal crevices, the very secrets of his heart. Slaveholders ever underrate the intelligence with which they have to grapple. I really understood the old man's mutterings, attitudes and gestures, about as well as he did himself. But slaveholders never encourage that kind of communication, with the slaves, by which they might learn to measure the depths of his knowledge. Ignorance is a high virtue in a human chattel; and as the master studies to keep the slave ignorant, the slave is cunning enough to make the master think he succeeds.

The slave fully appreciates the saying, "where ignorance is bliss, 'tis folly to be wise." When old master's gestures were violent, ending with a threatening shake of the head, and a sharp snap of his middle finger and thumb, I deemed it wise to keep at a respectable distance from him; for, at such times, trifling faults stood, in his eyes, as momentous offenses; and, having both the power and the disposition, the victim had only to be near him to catch the punishment, deserved or undeserved.

One of the first circumstances that opened my eyes to the cruelty and wickedness of slavery, and the heartlessness of my old master, was the refusal of the latter to interpose his authority, to protect and shield a young woman, who had been most cruelly abused and beaten by his overseer in Tuckahoe. This overseer—a Mr. Plummer—was a man like most of his class, little better than a human brute; and, in addition to his general profligacy and repulsive coarseness, the creature was a miserable drunkard. He was, probably, employed by my old master, less on account of the excellence of his services, than for the cheap rate at which they could be obtained. He was not fit to have the management of a drove of mules. In a fit of drunken madness, he committed the outrage which brought the young woman in question down to my old master's for protection.

This young woman was the daughter of Milly, an own aunt of mine. The poor girl, on arriving at our house, presented a pitiable appearance. She had left in haste, and without preparation; and, probably, without the knowledge of Mr. Plummer. She had traveled twelve miles, bare-footed, bare-necked and bare-headed. Her neck and shoulders were covered with scars, newly made; and not content with marring her neck and shoulders, with the cowhide, the cowardly brute had dealt her a blow on the head with a hickory club, which cut a horrible gash, and left her face literally covered with blood. In this condition, the poor young woman came down, to implore protection at the hands of my old master. I expected to see him boil over with rage at the revolting deed, and to hear him fill the air with curses upon the brutal Plummer; but I was disappointed.

He sternly told her, in an angry tone, he "believed she deserved every bit of it," and, if she did not go home instantly, he would himself take the remaining skin from her neck and back. Thus was the poor girl compelled to return, without redress, and perhaps to receive an additional flogging for daring to appeal to old master against the overseer.

Old master seemed furious at the thought of being troubled by such complaints. I did not, at that time, understand the philosophy of his treatment of my cousin. It was stern, unnatural, violent. Had the man no bowels of compassion? Was he dead to all sense of humanity? No. I think I now understand it. This treatment is a part of the system, rather than a part of the man. Were slaveholders to listen to complaints of this sort against the overseers, the luxury of owning large numbers of slaves, would be impossible. It would do away with the office of overseer, entirely; or, in other words, it would convert the master himself into an overseer. It would occasion great loss of time and labor, leaving the overseer in fetters, and without the necessary power to secure obedience to his orders. A privilege so dangerous as that of appeal, is, therefore, strictly prohibited; and anyone exercising it, runs a fearful hazard.

Nevertheless, when a slave has nerve enough to exercise it, and boldly approaches his master, with a well-founded complaint against an overseer, though he may be repulsed, and may even have that of which he complains repeated at the time, and, though he may be beaten by his master, as well as by the overseer, for his temerity, in the end the policy of complaining is, generally, vindicated by the relaxed rigor of the overseer's treatment. The latter becomes more careful, and less disposed to use the lash upon such slaves thereafter. It is with this final result in view, rather than with any expectation of immediate good, that the outraged slave is induced to meet his master with a complaint. The overseer very naturally dislikes to have the ear of the master disturbed by complaints; and, either upon this consideration, or upon advice and warning privately given him by his employers, he generally modifies the rigor of his rule, after an outbreak of the kind to which I have been referring.

Howsoever the slaveholder may allow himself to act toward his slave, and, whatever cruelty he may deem it wise, for example's sake, or for the gratification of his humor, to inflict, he cannot, in the absence of all provocation, look with pleasure upon the bleeding wounds of a defenseless slave-woman. When he drives her from his presence without redress, or the hope of redress, he acts, generally, from motives of policy, rather than from a hardened nature, or from innate brutality. Yet, let but his own temper be stirred, his own passions get loose, and the slave-owner will go far beyond the overseer in cruelty. He will convince the slave that his wrath is far more terrible and boundless, and vastly more to be dreaded, than that of the underling overseer. What may have been mechanically and heartlessly done by the overseer, is now done with a will. The man who now wields the lash is irresponsible. He may, if he pleases, cripple or kill, without fear of consequences; except in so far as it may concern profit or loss. To a man of violent temper—as my old master was—this was but a very slender and inefficient restraint. I have seen him in a tempest of passion, such as I have just described—a passion into which entered all the bitter ingredients of pride, hatred, envy, jealousy, and the thirst for revenge.

The circumstances which I am about to narrate, and which gave rise to this fearful tempest of passion, are not singular nor isolated in slave life, but are common in every slaveholding community in which I have lived. They are incidental to the relation of master and slave, and exist in all sections of slave- holding countries.

The reader will have noticed that, in enumerating the names of the slaves who lived with my old master, Esther is mentioned. This was a young woman who possessed that which is ever a curse to the slave-girl; namely — personal beauty. She was tall, well formed, and made a fine appearance. The daughters of Col. Lloyd could scarcely surpass her in personal charms. Esther was courted by Ned Roberts, and he was as fine looking a young man, as she was a woman. He was the son of a favorite slave of Col. Lloyd. Some slaveholders would have been glad to promote the marriage of two such persons; but, for some reason or other, my old master took it upon him to break up the growing intimacy between Esther and Edward. He strictly ordered her to quit the company of said Roberts, telling her that he would punish her severely if he ever found her again in Edward's company. This unnatural and heartless order was, of course, broken. A woman's love is not to be annihilated by the peremptory command of anyone, whose breath is in his nostrils.

It was impossible to keep Edward and Esther apart. Meet they would, and meet they did. Had old master been a man of honor and purity, his motives, in this matter, might have been viewed more favorably. As it was, his motives were as abhorrent, as his methods were foolish and contemptible. It was too evident that he was not concerned for the girl's welfare. It is one of the damning characteristics of the slave system, that it robs its victims of every earthly incentive to a holy life. The fear of God, and the hope of heaven, are found sufficient to sustain many slave-women, amidst the snares and dangers of their strange lot; but, this side of God and heaven, a slave-woman is at the mercy of the power, caprice and passion of her owner.

Slavery provides no means for the honorable continuance of the race. Marriage as imposing obligations on the parties to it—has no existence here, except in such hearts as purer and higher than the standard morality around them. It is one of the consolations of my life, that I know of many honorable instances of persons who maintained their honor, where all around was corrupt.

Esther was evidently much attached to Edward, and abhorred—as she had reason to do—the tyrannical and base behavior of old master. Edward was young, and fine looking, and he loved and courted her. He might have been her husband, in the high sense just alluded to; but WHO and what was this old master? His attentions were plainly brutal and selfish, and it was as natural that Esther should loathe him, as that she should love Edward. Abhorred and circumvented as he was, old master, having the power, very easily took revenge.

I happened to see this exhibition of his rage and cruelty toward Esther. The time selected was singular. It was early in the morning, when all besides was still, and before any of the family, in the house or kitchen, had left their beds. I saw but few of the shocking preliminaries, for the cruel work had begun before I awoke. I was probably awakened by the shrieks and piteous cries of poor Esther. My sleeping place was on the floor of a little, rough closet, which opened into the kitchen; and through the cracks of its unplanted boards, I could distinctly see and hear what was going on, without being seen by old master.

Esther's wrists were firmly tied, and the twisted rope was fastened to a strong staple in a heavy wooden joist above, near the fireplace. Here she stood, on a bench, her arms tightly drawn over her breast. Her back and shoulders were bare to the waist. Behind her stood old master, with cowskin in hand, preparing his barbarous work with all manner of harsh, coarse, and tantalizing epithets. The screams of his victim were most piercing. He was cruelly deliberate, and protracted the torture, as one who was delighted with the scene. Again and again he drew the hateful whip through his hand, adjusting it with a view of dealing the most pain-giving blow. Poor Esther had never yet been severely whipped, and her shoulders were plump and tender. Each blow, vigorously laid on, brought screams as well as blood. "Have mercy; Oh! have mercy" she cried; "I won't do so no more;" but her piercing cries seemed only to increase his fury. His answers to them are too coarse and blasphemous to be produced here. The whole scene, with all its attendants, was revolting and shocking, to the last degree; and when the motives of this brutal castigation are considered,—language has no power to convey a just sense of its awful criminality.

After laying on some thirty or forty stripes, old master untied his suffering victim, and let her get down. She could scarcely stand, when untied. From my heart I pitied her, and—child though I was—the outrage kindled in me a feeling far from peaceful; but I was hushed, terrified, stunned, and could do nothing, and the fate of Esther might be mine next. The scene here described was often repeated in the case of poor Esther, and her life, as I knew it, was one of wretchedness.

6

Things I saw

The heart-rending incidents, related in the foregoing chapter, led me, thus early, to inquire into the nature and history of slavery. **Why am I a slave? Why are some people slaves, and others masters? Was there ever a time this was not so? How did the relation commence?**

These were the perplexing questions which began now to claim my thoughts, and to exercise the weak powers of my mind, for I was still but a child, and knew less than children of the same age in the free states. As my questions concerning these things were only put to children a little older, and little better informed than myself, I was not rapid in reaching a solid footing. By some means I learned from these inquiries that "God, up in the sky," made everybody; and that he made white people to be masters and mistresses, and black people to be slaves. This did not satisfy me, nor lessen my interest in the subject. I was told, too, that God was good, and that He knew what was best for me, and best for everybody. This was less satisfactory than the first statement; because it came, point blank, against all my notions of goodness. It was not good to let old master cut the flesh off Esther, and make her cry so. Besides, how did people know that God made black people to be slaves? Did they go up in the sky and learn it? or, did He come down and tell them so? All was dark here. It was some relief to my hard notions of the goodness of God, that, although he made white men to be slaveholders, he did not make them to be bad slaveholders, and that, in due time, he would punish the bad slaveholders; that he would, when they died, send them to the bad place, where they would be "burnt up." Nevertheless, I could not reconcile the relation of slavery with my crude notions of goodness.

Then, too, I found that there were puzzling exceptions to this theory of slavery on both sides, and in the middle. I knew of blacks who were not slaves; I knew of whites who were not slaveholders; and I knew of persons who were nearly white, who were slaves. Color, therefore, was a very unsatisfactory basis for slavery.

Once, however, engaged in the inquiry, I was not very long in finding out the true solution of the matter. It was not color, but crime, not God, but man, that afforded the true explanation of the existence of slavery; nor was I long in finding out another important truth, viz: what man can make, man can unmake. The appalling darkness faded away, and I was master of the subject. There were slaves here, direct from Guinea; and there were many who could say that their fathers and mothers were stolen from Africa—forced from their homes, and compelled to serve as slaves. This, to me, was knowledge; but it was a kind of knowledge which filled me with a burning hatred of slavery, increased my suffering, and left me without the means of breaking away from my bondage. Yet it was knowledge quite worth possessing. I could not have been more than seven or eight years old, when I began to make this subject my study. It was with me in the woods and fields; along the shore of the river, and wherever my boyish wanderings led me; and though I was, at that time, quite ignorant of the existence of the free states, I distinctly remember being, even then, most strongly impressed with the idea of being a freeman some day. This cheering assurance was an inborn dream of my human nature a constant menace to slavery—and one which all the powers of slavery were unable to silence or extinguish.

Up to the time of the brutal flogging of my Aunt Esther—for she was my own aunt—and the horrid plight in which I had seen my cousin from Tuckahoe, who had been so badly beaten by the cruel Mr. Plummer, my attention had not been called, especially, to the gross features of slavery. I had, of course, heard of whippings and of savage rencontres between overseers and slaves, but I had always been out of the way at the times and places of their occurrence. My plays and sports, most of the time, took me from the corn and tobacco fields, where the great body of the hands were at work, and where scenes of cruelty were enacted and witnessed. But, after the whipping of Aunt Esther, I saw many cases of the same shocking nature, not only in my master's house, but on Col. Lloyd's plantation.

One of the first which I saw, and which greatly agitated me, was the whipping of a woman belonging to Col. Lloyd, named Nelly. The offense alleged against Nelly, was one of the commonest and most indefinite in the whole catalogue of offenses usually laid to the charge of slaves, viz: "impudence." This may mean almost anything, or nothing at all, just according to the caprice of the master or overseer, at the moment. But, whatever it is, or is not, if it gets the name of "impudence," the party charged with it is sure of a flogging. This offense may be committed in various ways; in the tone of an answer; in answering at all; in not answering; in the expression of countenance; in the motion of the head; in the gait, manner and bearing of the slave. In the case under consideration, I can easily believe that, according to all slaveholding standards, here was a genuine instance of impudence. In Nelly there were all the necessary conditions for committing the offense.

She was a bright mulatto, the recognized wife of a favorite "hand" on board Col. Lloyd's sloop, and the mother of five sprightly children. She was a vigorous and spirited woman, and one of the most likely, on the plantation, to be guilty of impudence. My attention was called to the scene, by the noise, curses and screams that proceeded from it; and, on going a little in that direction, I came upon the parties engaged in the skirmish. Mr. Siever, the overseer, had hold of Nelly, when I caught sight of them; he was endeavoring to drag her toward a tree, which endeavor Nelly was sternly resisting; but to no purpose, except to retard the progress of the overseer's plans.

Nelly—as I have said—was the mother of five children; three of them were present, and though quite small (from seven to ten years old, I should think) they gallantly came to their mother's defense, and gave the overseer an excellent pelting with stones. One of the little fellows ran up, seized the overseer by the leg and bit him; but the monster was too busily engaged with Nelly, to pay any attention to the assaults of the children. There were numerous bloody marks on Mr. Sevier's face, when I first saw him, and they increased as the struggle went on. The imprints of Nelly's fingers were visible, and I was glad to see them. Amidst the wild screams of the children—"Let my mammy go"—"let my mammy go"—there escaped, from between the teeth of the bullet-headed overseer, a few bitter curses, mingled with threats, that "he would teach the d—d b—h how to give a white man impudence."

There is no doubt that Nelly felt herself superior, in some respects, to the slaves around her. She was a wife and a mother; her husband was a valued and favorite slave. Besides, he was one of the first hands on board of the sloop, and the sloop hands—since they had to represent the plantation abroad—were generally treated tenderly. The overseer never was allowed to whip Harry; why then should he be allowed to whip Harry's wife? Thoughts of this kind, no doubt, influenced her; but, for whatever reason, she nobly resisted, and, unlike most of the slaves, seemed determined to make her whipping cost Mr. Sevier as much as possible. The blood on his (and her) face, attested her skill, as well as her courage and dexterity in using her nails. Maddened by her resistance, I expected to see Mr. Sevier level her to the ground by a stunning blow; but no; like a savage bull-dog—which he resembled both in temper and appearance—he maintained his grip, and steadily dragged his victim toward the tree, disregarding alike her blows, and the cries of the children for their mother's release. He would, doubtless, have knocked her down with his hickory stick, but that such act might have cost him his place. It is often deemed advisable to knock a man slave down, in order to tie him, but it is considered cowardly and inexcusable, in an overseer, thus to deal with a woman. He is expected to tie her up, and to give her what is called, in southern parlance, a "genteel flogging," without any very great outlay of strength or skill.

I watched, with palpitating interest, the course of the preliminary struggle, and was saddened by every new advantage gained over her by the ruffian. There were times when she seemed likely to get the better of the brute, but he finally overpowered her, and succeeded in getting his rope around her arms, and in firmly tying her to the tree, at which he had been aiming. This done, and Nelly was at the mercy of his merciless lash; and now, what followed, I have no heart to describe. The cowardly creature made good his every threat; and wielded the lash with all the hot zest of furious revenge. The cries of the woman, while undergoing the terrible infliction, were mingled with those of the children, sounds which I hope the reader may never be called upon to hear. When Nelly was untied, her back was covered with blood. The red stripes were all over her shoulders. She was whipped— severely whipped; but she was not subdued, for she continued to denounce the overseer, and to call him every vile name. He had bruised her flesh, but had left her invincible spirit undaunted. Such floggings are seldom repeated by the same overseer. They prefer to whip those who are most easily whipped. The old doctrine that submission is the very best cure for outrage and wrong, does not hold good on the slave plantation. He is whipped oftenest, who is whipped easiest; and that slave who has the courage to stand up for himself against the overseer, although he may have many hard stripes at the first, becomes, in the end, a freeman, even though he sustain the formal relation of a slave.

"You can shoot me but you can't whip me," said a slave to Rigby Hopkins; and the result was that he was neither whipped nor shot. If the latter had been his fate, it would have been less deplorable than the living and lingering death to which cowardly and slavish souls are subjected. I do not know that Mr. Sevier ever undertook to whip Nelly again. He probably never did, for it was not long after his attempt to subdue her, that he was taken sick, and died. The wretched man died as he had lived, unrepentant; and it was said—with how much truth I know not—that in the very last hours of his life, his ruling passion showed itself, and that when wrestling with death, he was uttering horrid oaths, and flourishing the cowskin, as though he was tearing the flesh off some helpless slave.

One thing is certain, that when he was in health, it was enough to chill the blood, and to stiffen the hair of an ordinary man, to hear Mr. Sevier talk. Nature, or his cruel habits, had given to his face an expression of unusual savageness, even for a slave-driver. Tobacco and rage had worn his teeth short, and nearly every sentence that escaped their compressed grating, was commenced or concluded with some outburst of profanity. His presence made the field alike the field of blood, and of blasphemy. Hated for his cruelty, despised for his cowardice, his death was deplored by no one outside his own house—if indeed it was deplored there; it was regarded by the slaves as a merciful interposition of Providence. Never went there a man to the grave loaded with heavier curses.

Mr. Sevier's place was promptly taken by a Mr. Hopkins, and the change was quite a relief, he being a very different man. He was, in all respects, a better man than his predecessor; as good as any man can be, and yet be an overseer. His course was characterized by no extraordinary cruelty; and when he whipped a slave, as he sometimes did, he seemed to take no especial pleasure in it, but, on the contrary, acted as though he felt it to be a mean business. Mr. Hopkins stayed but a short time; his place much to the regret of the slaves generally—was taken by a Mr. Gore, of whom more will be said hereafter. It is enough, for the present, to say, that he was no improvement on Mr. Sevier, except that he was less noisy and less profane.

I have already referred to the business-like aspect of Col. Lloyd's plantation. This business-like appearance was much increased on the two days at the end of each month, when the slaves from the different farms came to get their monthly allowance of meal and meat. These were gala days for the slaves, and there was much rivalry among them as to who should be elected to go up to the great house farm for the allowance, and, indeed, to attend to any business at this (for them) the capital. The beauty and grandeur of the place, its numerous slave population, and the fact that Harry, Peter and Jake the sailors of the sloop—almost always kept, privately, little trinkets which they bought at Baltimore, to sell, made it a privilege to come to the great house farm. Being selected, too, for this office, was deemed a high honor. It was taken as a proof of confidence and favor; but, probably, the chief motive of the competitors for the place, was, a desire to break the dull monotony of the field, and to get beyond the overseer's eye and lash.

Once on the road with an ox team, and seated on the tongue of his cart, with no overseer to look after him, the slave was comparatively free; and, if thoughtful, he had time to think. Slaves are generally expected to sing as well as to work. A silent slave is not liked by masters or overseers.

"Make a noise," "make a noise," and "bear a hand," are the words usually addressed to the slaves when there is silence amongst them. This may account for the almost constant singing heard in the southern states. There was, generally, more or less singing among the teamsters, as it was one means of letting the overseer know where they were, and that they were moving on with the work. But, on allowance day, those who visited the great house farm were peculiarly excited and noisy. While on their way, they would make the dense old woods, for miles around, reverberate with their wild notes. These were not always merry because they were wild. On the contrary, they were mostly of a plaintive cast, and told a tale of grief and sorrow. In the most boisterous outbursts of rapturous sentiment, there was ever a tinge of deep melancholy.

I have never heard any songs like those anywhere since I left slavery, except when in Ireland. There I heard the same wailing notes, and was much affected by them. It was during the famine of 1845-6. In all the songs of the slaves, there was ever some expression in praise of the great house farm; something which would flatter the pride of the owner, and, possibly, draw a favorable glance from him.

I am going away to the great house farm,
O yea! O yea! O yea!
My old master is a good old master,
O yea! O yea! O yea!

This they would sing, with other words of their own improvising—jargon to others, but full of meaning to themselves. I have sometimes thought, that the mere hearing of those songs would do more to impress truly spiritual-minded men and women with the soul-crushing and death-dealing character of slavery, than the reading of whole volumes of its mere physical cruelties. They speak to the heart and to the soul of the thoughtful. I cannot better express my sense of them now, than ten years ago, when, in sketching my life, I thus spoke of this feature of my plantation experience:

I did not, when a slave, understand the deep meanings of those rude, and apparently incoherent songs. I was myself within the circle, so that I neither saw or heard as those without might see and hear. They told a tale which was then altogether beyond my feeble comprehension; they were tones, loud, long and deep, breathing the prayer and complaint of souls boiling over with the bitterest anguish. Every tone was a testimony against slavery, and a prayer to God for deliverance from chains. The hearing of those wild notes always depressed my spirits, and filled my heart with ineffable sadness. The mere recurrence, even now, afflicts my spirit, and while I am writing these lines, my tears are falling. To those songs I trace my first glimmering conceptions of the dehumanizing character of slavery. I can never get rid of that conception. Those songs still follow me, to deepen my hatred of slavery, and quicken my sympathies for my brethren in bonds. If any one wishes to be impressed with a sense of the soul-killing power of slavery, let him go to Col. Lloyd's plantation, and, on allowance day, place himself in the deep, pine woods, and there let him, in silence, thoughtfully analyze the sounds that shall pass through the chambers of his soul, and if he is not thus impressed, it will only be because "there is no flesh in his obdurate heart."

The remark is not infrequently made, that slaves are the most contended and happy laborers in the world. They dance and sing, and make all manner of joyful noises—so they do; but it is a great mistake to suppose them happy because they sing. The songs of the slave represent the sorrows, rather than the joys, of his heart; and he is relieved by them, only as an aching heart is relieved by its tears. Such is the constitution of the human mind, that, when pressed to extremes, it often avails itself of the most opposite methods. Extremes meet in mind as in matter. When the slaves on board of the "Pearl" were overtaken, arrested, and carried to prison—their hopes for freedom blasted—as they marched in chains they sang, and found (as Emily Edmunson tells us) a melancholy relief in singing. The singing of a man cast away on a desolate island, might be as appropriately considered an evidence of his contentment and happiness, as the singing of a slave. Sorrow and desolation have their songs, as well as joy and peace. Slaves sing more to make themselves happy, than to express their happiness.

It is the boast of slaveholders, that their slaves enjoy more of the physical comforts of life than the peasantry of any country in the world. My experience contradicts this. The men and the women slaves on Col. Lloyd's farm, received, as their monthly allowance of food, eight pounds of pickled pork, or their equivalent in fish. The pork was often tainted, and the fish was of the poorest quality—herrings, which would bring very little if offered for sale in any northern market. With their pork or fish, they had one bushel of Indian meal—unbolted—of which quite fifteen per cent was fit only to feed pigs. With this, one pint of salt was given; and this was the entire monthly allowance of a full grown slave, working constantly in the open field, from morning until night, every day in the month except Sunday, and living on a fraction more than a quarter of a pound of meat per day, and less than a peck of cornmeal per week.

There is no kind of work that a man can do which requires a better supply of food to prevent physical exhaustion, than the field-work of a slave. So much for the slave's allowance of food; now for his raiment. The yearly allowance of clothing for the slaves on this plantation, consisted of two tow-linen shirts—such linen as the coarsest crash towels are made of; one pair of trousers of the same material, for summer, and a pair of trousers and a jacket of woolen, most lazily put together, for winter; one pair of yarn stockings, and one pair of shoes of the coarsest description.

The slave's entire apparel could not have cost more than eight dollars per year. The allowance of food and clothing for the little children, was committed to their mothers, or to the older slave women having the care of them. Children who were unable to work in the field, had neither shoes, stockings, jackets nor trousers given them. Their clothing consisted of two coarse tow-linen shirts—already described—per year; and when these failed them, as they often did, they went naked until the next allowance day. Flocks of little children from five to ten years old, might be seen on Col. Lloyd's plantation, as destitute of clothing as any little heathen on the west coast of Africa; and this, not merely during the summer months, but during the frosty weather of March. The little girls were no better off than the boys; all were nearly in a state of nudity.

As to beds to sleep on, they were known to none of the field hands; nothing but a coarse blanket—not so good as those used in the north to cover horses—was given them, and this only to the men and women. The children stuck themselves in holes and corners, about the quarters; often in the corner of the huge chimneys, with their feet in the ashes to keep them warm. The want of beds, however, was not considered a very great privation. Time to sleep was of far greater importance, for, when the day's work is done, most of the slaves have their washing, mending and cooking to do; and, having few or none of the ordinary facilities for doing such things, very many of their sleeping hours are consumed in necessary preparations for the duties of the coming day.

The sleeping apartments—if they may be called such—have little regard to comfort or decency. Old and young, male and female, married and single, drop down upon the common clay floor, each covering up with his or her blanket,—the only protection they have from cold or exposure. The night, however, is shortened at both ends. The slaves work often as long as they can see, and are late in cooking and mending for the coming day; and, at the first gray streak of morning, they are summoned to the field by the driver's horn.

More slaves are whipped for oversleeping than for any other fault. Neither age nor sex finds any favor. The overseer stands at the quarter door, armed with stick and cowskin, ready to whip any who may be a few minutes behind time. When the horn is blown, there is a rush for the door, and the hinder-most one is sure to get a blow from the overseer. Young mothers who worked in the field, were allowed an hour, about ten o'clock in the morning, to go home to nurse their children. Sometimes they were compelled to take their children with them, and to leave them in the corner of the fences, to prevent loss of time in nursing them.

The overseer generally rides about the field on horseback. A cowskin and a hickory stick are his constant companions. The cowskin is a kind of whip seldom seen in the northern states. It is made entirely of untanned, but dried, ox hide, and is about as hard as a piece of well-seasoned live oak. It is made of various sizes, but the usual length is about three feet. The part held in the hand is nearly an inch in thickness; and, from the extreme end of the butt or handle, the cowskin tapers its whole length to a point. This makes it quite elastic and springy. A blow with it, on the hardest back, will gash the flesh, and make the blood start. Cowskins are painted red, blue and green, and are the favorite slave whip. I think this whip worse than the "cat-o'nine-tails." It condenses the whole strength of the arm to a single point, and comes with a spring that makes the air whistle. It is a terrible instrument, and is so handy, that the overseer can always have it on his person, and ready for use. The temptation to use it is ever strong; and an overseer can, if disposed, always have cause for using it. With him, it is literally a word and a blow, and, in most cases, the blow comes first.

As a general rule, slaves do not come to the quarters for either breakfast or dinner, but take their "ash cake" with them, and eat it in the field. This was so on the home plantation; probably, because the distance from the quarter to the field, was sometimes two, and even three miles.

The dinner of the slaves consisted of a huge piece of ash cake, and a small piece of pork, or two salt herrings. Not having ovens, nor any suitable cooking utensils, the slaves mixed their meal with a little water, to such thickness that a spoon would stand erect in it; and, after the wood had burned away to coals and ashes, they would place the dough between oak leaves and lay it carefully in the ashes, completely covering it; hence, the bread is called ash cake. The surface of this peculiar bread is covered with ashes, to the depth of a sixteenth part of an inch, and the ashes, certainly, do not make it very grateful to the teeth, nor render it very palatable. The bran, or coarse part of the meal, is baked with the fine, and bright scales run through the bread.

This bread, with its ashes and bran, would disgust and choke a northern man, but it is quite liked by the slaves. They eat it with avidity, and are more concerned about the quantity than about the quality. They are far too scantily provided for, and are worked too steadily, to be much concerned for the quality of their food. The few minutes allowed them at dinner time, after partaking of their coarse repast, are variously spent. Some lie down on the "turning row," and go to sleep; others draw together, and talk; and others are at work with needle and thread, mending their tattered garments. Sometimes you may hear a wild, hoarse laugh arise from a circle, and often a song. Soon, however, the overseer comes dashing through the field. "Tumble up! Tumble up, and to work, work," is the cry; and, now, from twelve o'clock (midday) till dark, the human cattle are in motion, wielding their clumsy hoes; hurried on by no hope of reward, no sense of gratitude, no love of children, no prospect of bettering their condition; nothing, save the dread and terror of the slave-driver's lash. So goes one day, and so comes and goes another.

But, let us now leave the rough usage of the field, where vulgar coarseness and brutal cruelty spread themselves and flourish, rank as weeds in the tropics; where a vile wretch, in the shape of a man, rides, walks, or struts about, dealing blows, and leaving gashes on broken-spirited men and helpless women, for thirty dollars per month—a business so horrible, hardening and disgraceful, that, rather, than engage in it, a decent man would blow his own brains out—and let the reader view with me the equally wicked, but less repulsive aspects of slave life; where pride and pomp roll luxuriously at ease; where the toil of a thousand men supports a single family in easy idleness and sin. This is the great house; it is the home of the LLOYDS!

Some idea of its splendor has already been given—and, it is here that we shall find that height of luxury which is the opposite of that depth of poverty and physical wretchedness that we have just now been contemplating. But, there is this difference in the two extremes; viz: that in the case of the slave, the miseries and hardships of his lot are imposed by others, and, in the master's case, they are imposed by himself. The slave is a subject, subjected by others; the slaveholder is a subject, but he is the author of his own subjection. There is more truth in the saying, that slavery is a greater evil to the master than to the slave, than many, who utter it, suppose. The self-executing laws of eternal justice follow close on the heels of the evil-doer here, as well as elsewhere; making escape from all its penalties impossible. But, let others philosophize; it is my province here to relate and describe; only allowing myself a word or two, occasionally, to assist the reader in the proper understanding of the facts narrated.

7

Life in the Great House

The close-fisted stinginess that fed the poor slave on coarse cornmeal and tainted meat; that clothed him in crashy tow-linen, and hurried him to toil through the field, in all weathers, with wind and rain beating through his tattered garments; that scarcely gave even the young slave-mother time to nurse her hungry infant in the fence corner; wholly vanishes on approaching the sacred precincts of the great house, the home of the Lloyds. There the scriptural phrase finds an exact illustration; the highly favored inmates of this mansion are literally arrayed "in purple and fine linen," and fare sumptuously every day!

The table groans under the heavy and blood-bought luxuries gathered with painstaking care, at home and abroad. Fields, forests, rivers and seas, are made tributary here. Immense wealth, and its lavish expenditure, fill the great house with all that can please the eye, or tempt the taste. Here, appetite, not food, is the great desideratum. Fish, flesh and fowl, are here in profusion. Chickens, of all breeds; ducks, of all kinds, wild and tame, the common, and the huge Muscovite; Guinea fowls, turkeys, geese, and pea fowls, are in their several pens, fat and fatting for the destined vortex. The graceful swan, the mongrels, the black-necked wild goose; partridges, quails, pheasants and pigeons; choice water fowl, with all their strange varieties, are caught in this huge family net. Beef, veal, mutton and venison, of the most select kinds and quality, roll bounteously to this grand consumer. The teeming riches of the Chesapeake bay, its rock, perch, drums, crocus, trout, oysters, crabs, and terrapin, are drawn hither to adorn the glittering table of the great house. The dairy, too, probably the finest on the Eastern Shore of Maryland—supplied by cattle of the best English stock, imported for the purpose, pours its rich donations of fragrant cheese, golden butter, and delicious cream, to heighten the attraction of the gorgeous, unending round of feasting.

Nor are the fruits of the earth forgotten or neglected. The fertile garden, many acres in size, constituting a separate establishment, distinct from the common farm—with its scientific gardener, imported from Scotland (a Mr. McDermott) with four men under his direction, was not behind, either in the abundance or in the delicacy of its contributions to the same full board. The tender asparagus, the succulent celery, and the delicate cauliflower; egg plants, beets, lettuce, parsnips, peas, and

French beans, early and late; radishes, cantaloupes, melons of all kinds; the fruits and flowers of all climes and of all descriptions, from the hardy apple of the north, to the lemon and orange of the south, culminated at this point. Baltimore gathered figs, raisins, almonds and juicy grapes from Spain. Wines and brandies from France; teas of various flavor from China; and rich, aromatic coffee from Java, all conspired to swell the tide of high life, where pride and indolence rolled and lounged in magnificence and satiety.

Behind the tall-backed and elaborately wrought chairs, stand the servants, men and maidens—fifteen in number —discriminately selected, not only with a view to their industry and faithfulness, but with special regard to their personal appearance, their graceful agility and captivating address. Some of these are armed with fans, and are fanning reviving breezes toward the over-heated brows of the alabaster ladies; others watch with eager eye, and with fawn-like step anticipate and supply wants before they are sufficiently formed to be announced by word or sign.

These servants constituted a sort of black aristocracy on Col. Lloyd's plantation. They resembled the field hands in nothing, except in color, and in this they held the advantage of a velvet-like glossiness, rich and beautiful. The hair, too, showed the same advantage. The delicate colored maid rustled in the scarcely worn silk of her young mistress, while the servant men were equally well attired from the over-flowing wardrobe of their young masters; so that, in dress, as well as in form and feature, in manner and speech, in tastes and habits, the distance between these favored few, and the sorrow and hunger-smitten multitudes of the quarter and the field, was immense; and this is seldom passed over.

Let us now glance at the stables and the carriage house, and we shall find the same evidences of pride and luxurious extravagance. Here are three splendid coaches, soft within and lustrous without. Here, too, are gigs, phaetons, barouches, sulkeys and sleighs. Here are saddles and harnesses—beautifully wrought and silver mounted—kept with every care. In the stable you will find, kept only for pleasure, full thirty-five horses, of the most approved blood for speed and beauty. There are two men here constantly employed in taking care of these horses. One of these men must be always in the stable, to answer every call from the great house. Over the way from the stable, is a house built expressly for the hounds —a pack of twenty-five or thirty—whose fare would have made glad the heart of a dozen slaves. Horses and hounds are not the only consumers of the slave's toil. There was practiced, at the Lloyd's, a hospitality which would have astonished and charmed any health-seeking northern divine or merchant, who might have chanced to share it. Viewed from his own table, and not from the field, the colonel was a model of generous hospitality. His house was, literally, a hotel, for weeks during the summer months. At these times, especially, the air was freighted with the rich fumes of baking, boiling, roasting and broiling.

The odors I shared with the winds; but the meats were under a more stringent monopoly except that, occasionally, I got a cake from Mas' Daniel. In Mas' Daniel I had a friend at court, from whom I learned many things which my eager curiosity was excited to know. I always knew when company was expected, and who they were, although I was an outsider, being the property, not of Col. Lloyd, but of a servant of the wealthy colonel. On these occasions, all that pride, taste and money could do, to dazzle and charm, was done.

Who could say that the servants of Col. Lloyd were not well clad and cared for, after witnessing one of his magnificent entertainments? Who could say that they did not seem to glory in being the slaves of such a master? Who, but a fanatic, could get up any sympathy for persons whose every movement was agile, easy and graceful, and who evinced a consciousness of high superiority? And who would ever venture to suspect that Col. Lloyd was subject to the troubles of ordinary mortals? Master and slave seem alike in their glory here? Can it all be seeming? Alas! it may only be a sham at last! This immense wealth; this gilded splendor; this profusion of luxury; this exemption from toil; this life of ease; this sea of plenty; aye, what of it all? Are the pearly gates of happiness and sweet content flung open to such suitors? Far from it!

I had excellent opportunities of witnessing the restless discontent and the capricious irritation of the Lloyds. My fondness for horses—not peculiar to me more than to other boys, attracted me, much of the time, to the stables. This establishment was especially under the care of "old" and "young" Barney—father and son. Old Barney was a fine looking old man, of a brownish complexion, who was quite portly, and wore a dignified aspect for a slave. He was, evidently, much devoted to his profession, and held his office an honorable one. He was a farrier as well as an ostler; he could bleed, remove lampers from the mouths of the horses, and was well instructed in horse medicines. No one on the farm knew, so well as Old Barney, what to do with a sick horse. But his gifts and acquirements were of little advantage to him. His office was by no means an enviable one. He often got presents, but he got stripes as well; for in nothing was Col. Lloyd more unreasonable and exacting, than in respect to the management of his pleasure horses. Any supposed inattention to these animals were sure to be visited with degrading punishment. His horses and dogs fared better than his men. Their beds must be softer and cleaner than those of his human cattle. No excuse could shield Old Barney, if the colonel only suspected something wrong about his horses; and, consequently, he was often punished when faultless.

It was absolutely painful to listen to the many unreasonable and fretful scoldings, poured out at the stable, by Col. Lloyd, his sons and sons-in-law. Of the latter, he had three—Messrs. Nicholson, Winder and Lownes. These all lived at the great house a portion of the year, and enjoyed the luxury of whipping the servants when they pleased, which was by no means infrequently. A horse was seldom brought out of the stable to which no objection could be raised. "There was dust in his hair;" "there was a twist in his reins;" "his mane did not lie straight;" "he had not been properly grained;" "his head did not look well;" "his foretop was not combed out;" "his fetlocks had not been properly trimmed;" something was always wrong. Listening to complaints, however groundless, Barney must stand, hat in hand, lips sealed, never answering a word. He must make no reply, no explanation; the judgment of the master must be deemed infallible, for his power is absolute and irresponsible. In a free state, a master, thus complaining without cause, of his ostler, might be told—"Sir, I am sorry I cannot please you, but, since I have done the best I can, your remedy is to dismiss me." Here, however, the ostler must stand, listen and tremble.

One of the most heart-saddening and humiliating scenes I ever witnessed, was the whipping of Old Barney, by Col. Lloyd himself. Here were two men, both advanced in years; there were the silvery locks of Col. L., and there was the bald and toil-worn brow of Old Barney; master and slave; superior and inferior here, but equals at the bar of God; and, in the common course of events, they must both soon meet in another world, in a world where all distinctions, except those based on obedience and disobedience, are blotted out forever.

"Uncover your head!" said the imperious master; he was obeyed. "Take off your jacket, you old rascal!" and off came Barney's jacket. "Down on your knees!" down knelt the old man, his shoulders bare, his bald head glistening in the sun, and his aged knees on the cold, damp ground. In his humble and debasing attitude, the master—that master to whom he had given the best years and the best strength of his life—came forward, and laid on thirty lashes, with his horse whip. The old man bore it patiently, to the last, answering each blow with a slight shrug of the shoulders, and a groan. I cannot think that Col. Lloyd succeeded in marring the flesh of Old Barney very seriously, for the whip was a light, riding whip; but the spectacle of an aged man—a husband and a father—humbly kneeling before a worm of the dust, surprised and shocked me at the time; and since I have grown old enough to think on the wickedness of slavery, few facts have been of more value to me than this, to which I was a witness. It reveals slavery in its true color, and in its maturity of repulsive hatefulness. I owe it to truth, however, to say, that this was the first and the last time I ever saw Old Barney, or any other slave, compelled to kneel to receive a whipping.

I saw, at the stable, another incident, which I will relate, as it is illustrative of a phase of slavery to which I have already referred in another connection. Besides two other coachmen, Col. Lloyd owned one named William, who, strangely enough, was often called by his surname, Wilks, by white and colored people on the home plantation. Wilks was a very fine looking man. He was about as white as anybody on the plantation; and in manliness of form, and comeliness of features, he bore a very striking resemblance to Mr. Murray Lloyd. It was whispered, and pretty generally admitted as a fact, that William Wilks was a son of Col. Lloyd, by a highly favored slave-woman, who was still on the plantation. There were many reasons for believing this whisper, not only in William's appearance, but in the undeniable freedom which he enjoyed over all others, and his apparent consciousness of being something more than a slave to his master. It was notorious, too, that William had a deadly enemy in Murray Lloyd, whom he so much resembled, and that the latter greatly worried his father with importunities to sell William. Indeed, he gave his father no rest until he did sell him, to Austin Woldfolk, the great slave-trader at that time. Before selling him, however, Mr. L. tried what giving William a whipping would do, toward making things smooth; but this was a failure. It was a compromise, and defeated itself; for, immediately after the infliction, the heart-sickened colonel atoned to William for the abuse, by giving him a gold watch and chain. Another fact, somewhat curious, is, that though sold to the remorseless Woldfolk, taken in irons to Baltimore and cast into prison, with a view to being driven to the south, William, by some means— always a mystery to me—outbid all his purchasers, paid for himself, and now resides in Baltimore, a FREEMAN. Is there not room to suspect, that, as the gold watch was presented to atone for the whipping, a purse of gold was given him by the same hand, with which to effect his purchase, as an atonement for the indignity involved in selling his own flesh and blood. All the circumstances of William, on the great house farm, show him to have occupied a different position from the other slaves, and, certainly, there is nothing in the supposed hostility of slave-holders to amalgamation, to forbid the supposition that William Wilks was the son of Edward Lloyd.

Practical amalgamation is common in every neighborhood where I have been in slavery. Col. Lloyd was not in the way of knowing much of the real opinions and feelings of his slaves respecting him. The distance between him and them was far too great to admit of such knowledge. His slaves were so numerous, that he did not know them when he saw them. Nor, indeed, did all his slaves know him. In this respect, he was inconveniently rich. It is reported of him, that, while riding along the road one day, he met a colored man, and addressed him in the usual way of speaking to colored people on the public highways of the south: "Well, boy, who do you belong to?" "To Col. Lloyd," replied the slave. "Well, does the colonel treat you well?" "No, sir," was the ready reply. "What? does he work you too hard?" "Yes, sir." "Well, don't he give enough to eat?" "Yes, sir, he gives me enough, such as it is." The colonel, after ascertaining where the slave belonged, rode on; the slave also went on about his business, not dreaming that he had been conversing with his master. He thought, said and heard nothing more of the matter, until two or three weeks afterwards. The poor man was then informed by his overseer, that, for having found fault with his master, he was now to be sold to a Georgia trader. He was immediately chained and handcuffed; and thus, without a moment's warning he was snatched away, and forever sundered from his family and friends, by a hand more unrelenting than that of death. This is the penalty of telling the simple truth, in answer to a series of plain questions. It is partly in consequence of such facts, that slaves, when inquired of as to their condition and the character of their masters, almost invariably say they are contented, and that their masters are kind.

Slaveholders have been known to send spies among their slaves, to ascertain, if possible, their views and feelings in regard to their condition. The frequency of this had the effect to establish among the slaves the maxim, that a still tongue makes a wise head. They suppress the truth rather than take the consequence of telling it, and, in so doing, they prove themselves a part of the human family. If they have anything to say of their master, it is, generally, something in his favor, especially when speaking to strangers. I was frequently asked, while a slave, if I had a kind master, and I do not remember ever to have given a negative reply. Nor did I, when pursuing this course, consider myself as uttering what was utterly false; for I always measured the kindness of my master by the standard of kindness set up by slave-holders around us.

However, slaves are like other people, and imbibe similar prejudices. They are apt to think their condition better than that of others. Many, under the influence of this prejudice, think their own masters are better than the masters of other slaves; and this, too, in some cases, when the very reverse is true. Indeed, it is not uncommon for slaves even to fall out and quarrel among themselves about the relative kindness of their masters, contending for the superior goodness of his own over that of others.

At the very same time, they mutually execrate their masters, when viewed separately. It was so on our plantation. When Col. Lloyd's slaves met those of Jacob Jepson, they seldom parted without a quarrel about their masters; Col. Lloyd's slaves contending that he was the richest, and Mr. Jepson's slaves that he was the smartest man of the two. Col. Lloyd's slaves would boost his ability to buy and sell Jacob Jepson; Mr. Jepson's slaves would boast his ability to whip Col. Lloyd. These quarrels would almost always end in a fight between the parties; those that beat were supposed to have gained the point at issue. They seemed to think that the greatness of their masters was transferable to themselves. To be a SLAVE, was thought to be bad enough; but to be a poor man's slave, was deemed a disgrace, indeed.

8

A Chapter of Horrors

As I have already intimated elsewhere, the slaves on Col. Lloyd's plantation, whose hard lot, under Mr. Sevier, the reader has already noticed and deplored, were not permitted to enjoy the comparatively moderate rule of Mr. Hopkins. The latter was succeeded by a very different man. The name of the new overseer was Austin Gore. Upon this individual I would fix particular attention; for under his rule there was more suffering from violence and bloodshed than had—according to the older slaves ever been experienced before on this plantation.

I confess, I hardly know how to bring this man fitly before the reader. He was, it is true, an overseer, and possessed, to a large extent, the peculiar characteristics of his class; yet, to call him merely an overseer, would not give the reader a fair notion of the man. I speak of overseers as a class. They are such. They are as distinct from the slaveholding gentry of the south, as are the fish-women of Paris, and the coal-heavers of London, distinct from other members of society. They constitute a separate fraternity at the south, not less marked than is the fraternity of Park Lane bullies in New York. They have been arranged and classified by that great law of attraction, which determines the spheres and affinities of men; which ordains, that men, whose malign and brutal propensities predominate over their moral and intellectual endowments, shall, naturally, fall into those employments which promise the largest gratification to those predominating instincts or propensities.

The office of overseer takes this raw material of vulgarity and brutality, and stamps it as a distinct class of southern society. But, in this class, as in all other classes, there are characters of marked individuality, even while they bear a general resemblance to the mass. Mr. Gore was one of those, to whom a general characterization would do no manner of justice. He was an overseer; but he was something more.

With the malign and tyrannical qualities of an overseer, he combined something of the lawful master. He had the artfulness and the mean ambition of his class; but he was wholly free from the disgusting swagger and noisy bravado of his fraternity. There was an easy air of independence about him; a calm self-possession, and a sternness of glance, which might well daunt hearts less timid than those of poor slaves, accustomed from childhood and through life to cower before a driver's lash. The home plantation of Col. Lloyd afforded an ample field for the exercise of the qualifications for overseership, which he possessed in such an eminent degree.

Mr. Gore was one of those overseers, who could torture the slightest word or look into impudence; he had the nerve, not only to resent, but to punish, promptly and severely. He never allowed himself to be answered back, by a slave. In this, he was as lordly and as imperious as Col. Edward Lloyd, himself; acting always up to the maxim, practically maintained by slave-holders, that it is better that a dozen slaves suffer under the lash, without fault, than that the master or the overseer should seem to have been wrong in the presence of the slave. Everything must be absolute here. Guilty or not guilty, it is enough to be accused, to be sure of a flogging.

The very presence of this man Gore was painful, and I shunned him as I would have shunned a rattlesnake. His piercing, black eyes, and sharp, shrill voice, ever awakened sensations of terror among the slaves. For so young a man (I describe him as he was, twenty-five or thirty years ago) Mr. Gore was singularly reserved and grave in the presence of slaves. He indulged in no jokes, said no funny things, and kept his own counsels. Other overseers, how brutal soever they might be, were, at times, inclined to gain favor with the slaves, by indulging a little pleasantry; but Gore was never known to be guilty of any such weakness. He was always the cold, distant, unapproachable overseer of Col. Edward Lloyd's plantation, and needed no higher pleasure than was involved in a faithful discharge of the duties of his office.

When he whipped, he seemed to do so from a sense of duty, and feared no consequences. What Hopkins did reluctantly, Gore did with alacrity. There was a stern will, an iron-like reality, about this Gore, which would have easily made him the chief of a band of pirates, had his environments been favorable to such a course of life. All the coolness, savage barbarity and freedom from moral restraint, which are necessary in the character of a pirate-chief, centered, I think, in this man Gore. Among many other deeds of shocking cruelty which he perpetrated, while I was at Mr. Lloyd's, was the murder of a young colored man, named Denby.

He was sometimes called Bill Denby, or Demby; (I write from sound, and the sounds on Lloyd's plantation are not very certain.) I knew him well. He was a powerful young man, full of animal spirits, and, so far as I know, he was among the most valuable of Col. Lloyd's slaves. In something—I know not what—he offended this Mr. Austin Gore, and, in accordance with the custom of the latter, he undertook to flog him. He gave Denby but few stripes; the latter broke away from him and plunged into the creek, and, standing there to the depth of his neck in water, he refused to come out at the order of the overseer; whereupon, for this refusal, Gore shot him dead! It is said that Gore gave Denby three calls, telling him that if he did not obey the last call, he would shoot him. When the third call was given, Denby stood his ground firmly; and this raised the question, in the minds of the by-standing slaves—"Will he dare to shoot?" Mr. Gore, without further parley, and without making any further effort to induce Denby to come out of the water, raised his gun deliberately to his face, took deadly aim at his standing victim, and, in an instant, poor Denby was numbered with the dead. His mangled body sank out of sight, and only his warm, red blood marked the place where he had stood.

This devilish outrage, this fiendish murder, produced, as it was well calculated to do, a tremendous sensation. A thrill of horror flashed through every soul on the plantation, if I may except the guilty wretch who had committed the hell-black deed. While the slaves generally were panic-struck, and howling with alarm, the murderer himself was calm and collected, and appeared as though nothing unusual had happened. The atrocity roused my old master, and he spoke out, in reprobation of it; but the whole thing proved to be less than a nine days' wonder. Both Col. Lloyd and my old master arraigned Gore for his cruelty in the matter, but this amounted to nothing. His reply, or explanation—as I remember to have heard it at the time was, that the extraordinary expedient was demanded by necessity; that Denby had become unmanageable; that he had set a dangerous example to the other slaves; and that, without some such prompt measure as that to which he had resorted, were adopted, there would be an end to all rule and order on the plantation. That very convenient covert for all manner of cruelty and outrage that cowardly alarm-cry, that the slaves would "take the place," was pleaded, in extenuation of this revolting crime, just as it had been cited in defense of a thousand similar ones. He argued, that if one slave refused to be corrected, and was allowed to escape with his life, when he had been told that he should lose it if he persisted in his course, the other slaves would soon copy his example; the result of which would be, the freedom of the slaves, and the enslavement of the whites.

I have every reason to believe that Mr. Gore's defense, or explanation, was deemed satisfactory—at least to Col. Lloyd. He continued in his office on the plantation. His fame as an overseer went abroad, and his horrid crime was not even submitted to judicial investigation. The murder was committed in the presence of slaves, and they, of course, could neither institute a suit, nor testify against the murderer. His bare word would go further in a court of law, than the united testimony of ten thousand black witnesses.

All that Mr. Gore had to do, was to make his peace with Col. Lloyd. This done, and the guilty perpetrator of one of the most foul murders goes unwhipped of justice, and uncensured by the community in which he lives. Mr. Gore lived in St. Michael's, Talbot county, when I left Maryland; if he is still alive he probably yet resides there; and I have no reason to doubt that he is now as highly esteemed, and as greatly respected, as though his guilty soul had never been stained with innocent blood. I am well aware that what I have now written will by some be branded as false and malicious. It will be denied, not only that such a thing ever did transpire, as I have now narrated, but that such a thing could happen in Maryland. I can only say—believe it or not—that I have said nothing but the literal truth, gainsay it who may.

9

My personal experience

I have nothing cruel or shocking to relate of my own personal experience, while I remained on Col. Lloyd's plantation, at the home of my old master. An occasional cuff from Aunt Katy, and a regular whipping from old master, such as any heedless and mischievous boy might get from his father, is all that I can mention of this sort. I was not old enough to work in the field, and, there being little else than field work to perform, I had much leisure. The most I had to do was to drive up the cows in the evening, to keep the front yard clean, and to perform small errands for my young mistress, Lucretia Auld. I have reasons for thinking this lady was very kindly disposed toward me, and, although I was not often the object of her attention, I constantly regarded her as my friend, and was always glad when it was my privilege to do her a service. In a family where there was so much that was harsh, cold and indifferent, the slightest word or look of kindness passed, with me, for its full value.

Miss Lucretia—as we all continued to call her long after her marriage—had bestowed upon me such words and looks as taught me that she pitied me, if she did not love me. In addition to words and looks, she sometimes gave me a piece of bread and butter; a thing not set down in the bill of fare, and which must have been an extra ration, planned aside from either Aunt Katy or old master, solely out of the tender regard and friendship she had for me. Then, too, I one day got into the wars with Uncle Able's son, "Ike," and had got sadly worsted; in fact, the little rascal had struck me directly in the forehead with a sharp piece of cinder, fused with iron, from the old blacksmith's forge, which made a cross in my forehead very plainly to be seen now. The gash bled very freely, and I roared very loudly and betook myself home. The coldhearted Aunt Katy paid no attention either to my wound or my roaring, except to tell me it served me right; I had no business with Ike; it was good for me; I would now keep away "from dem Lloyd niggers."

Miss Lucretia, in this state of the case, came forward; and, in quite a different spirit from that manifested by Aunt Katy, she called me into the parlor (an extra privilege of itself) and, without us- ing toward me any of the hard-hearted and reproachful epithets of my kitchen tormentor, she quietly acted the good Samaritan. With her own soft hand she washed the blood from my head and face, fetched her own balsam bottle, and with the balsam wetted a nice piece of white linen, and bound up my head. The balsam was not more healing to the wound in my head, than her kindness was healing to the wounds in my spirit, made by the unfeeling words of Aunt Katy.

After this, Miss Lucretia was my friend. I felt her to be such; and I have no doubt that the simple act of binding up my head, did much to awaken in her mind an interest in my welfare. It is quite true, that this interest was never very marked, and it seldom showed itself in anything more than in giving me a piece of bread when I was hungry; but this was a great favor on a slave plantation, and I was the only one of the children to whom such attention was paid. When very hungry, I would go into the back yard and play under Miss Lucretia's window. When pretty severely pinched by hunger, I had a habit of singing, which the good lady very soon came to understand as a petition for a piece of bread. When I sung under Miss Lucretia's window, I was very apt to get well paid for my music. The reader will see that I now had two friends, both at important points—Mas' Daniel at the great house, and Miss Lucretia at home. From Mas' Daniel I got protection from the bigger boys; and from Miss Lucretia I got bread, by singing when I was hungry, and sympathy when I was abused by that termagant, who had the reins of government in the kitchen.

For such friendship I felt deeply grateful, and bitter as are my recollections of slavery, I love to recall any instances of kindness, any sunbeams of humane treatment, which found way to my soul through the iron grating of my house of bondage. Such beams seem all the brighter from the general darkness into which they penetrate, and the impression they make is vividly distinct and beautiful.

As I have before intimated, I was seldom whipped—and never severely—by my old master. I suffered little from the treatment I received, except from hunger and cold. These were my two great physical troubles. I could neither get a sufficiency of food nor of clothing; but I suffered less from hunger than from cold. In hottest summer and coldest winter, I was kept almost in a state of nudity; no shoes, no stockings, no jacket, no trousers; nothing but coarse sackcloth or tow-linen, made into a sort of shirt, reaching down to my knees. This I wore night and day, changing it once a week. In the day time I could protect myself pretty well, by keeping on the sunny side of the house; and in bad weather, in the corner of the kitchen chimney. The great difficulty was, to keep warm during the night. I had no bed. The pigs in the pen had leaves, and the horses in the stable had straw, but the children had no beds. They lodged anywhere in the ample kitchen. I slept, generally, in a little closet, without even a blanket to cover me. In very cold weather. I sometimes got down the bag in which corn meal was usually carried to the mill, and crawled into that. Sleeping there, with my head in and feet out, I was partly protected, though not comfortable. My feet have been so cracked with the frost, that the pen with which I am writing might be laid in the gashes.

The manner of taking our meals at old master's, indicated but little refinement. Our cornmeal mush, when sufficiently cooled, was placed in a large wooden tray, or trough, like those used in making maple sugar here in the north. This tray was set down, either on the floor of the kitchen, or out of doors on the ground; and the children were called, like so many pigs; and like so many pigs they would come, and literally devour the mush—some with oyster shells, some with pieces of shingles, and none with spoons. He that eat fastest got most, and he that was strongest got the best place; and few left the trough really satisfied. I was the most unlucky of any, for Aunt Katy had no good feeling for me; and if I pushed any of the other children, or if they told her anything unfavorable of me, she always believed the worst, and was sure to whip me.

As I grew older and more thoughtful, I was more and more filled with a sense of my wretchedness. The cruelty of Aunt Katy, the hunger and cold I suffered, and the terrible reports of wrong and outrage which came to my ear, together with what I almost daily witnessed, led me, when yet but eight or nine years old, to wish I had never been born. I used to contrast my condition with the black-birds, in whose wild and sweet songs I fancied them so happy! Their apparent joy only deepened the shades of my sorrow. There are thoughtful days in the lives of children—at least there were in mine when they grapple with all the great, primary subjects of knowledge, and reach, in a moment, conclusions which no subsequent experience can shake. I was just as well aware of the unjust, unnatural and murderous character of slavery, when nine years old, as I am now. Without any appeal to books, to laws, or to authorities of any kind, it was enough to accept God as a father, to regard slavery as a crime.

I was not ten years old when I left Col. Lloyd's plantation for Baltimore. I left that plantation with inexpressible joy. I never shall forget the ecstasy with which I received the intelligence from my friend, Miss Lucretia, that my old master had determined to let me go to Baltimore to live with Mr. Hugh Auld, a brother to Mr. Thomas Auld, my old master's son-in-law. I received this information about three days before my departure. They were three of the happiest days of my childhood. I spent the largest part of these three days in the creek, washing off the plantation scurf, and preparing for my new home. Mrs. Lucretia took a lively interest in getting me ready. She told me I must get all the dead skin off my feet and knees, before I could go to Baltimore, for the people there were very cleanly, and would laugh at me if I looked dirty; and, besides, she was intending to give me a pair of trousers, which I should not put on unless I got all the dirt off.

This was a warning to which I was bound to take heed; for the thought of owning a pair of trousers, was great, indeed. It was almost a sufficient motive, not only to induce me to scrub off the mange (as pig drovers would call it) but the skin as well. So I went at it in good earnest, working for the first time in the hope of reward. I was greatly excited, and could hardly consent to sleep, lest I should be left. The ties that, ordinarily, bind children to their homes, were all severed, or they never had any existence in my case, at least so far as the home plantation of Col. L. was concerned. I therefore found no severe trail at the moment of my departure, such as I had experienced when separated from my home in Tuckahoe. My home at my old master's was charmless to me; it was not home, but a prison to me; on parting from it, I could not feel that I was leaving anything which I could have enjoyed by staying.

My mother was now long dead; my grandmother was far away, so that I seldom saw her; Aunt Katy was my unrelenting tormentor; and my two sisters and brothers, owing to our early separation in life, and the family-destroying power of slavery, were, comparatively, strangers to me. The fact of our relationship was almost blotted out. I looked for home elsewhere, and was confident of finding none which I should relish less than the one I was leaving. If, however, I found in my new home to which I was going with such blissful anticipations—hardship, whipping and nakedness, I had the questionable consolation that I should not have escaped any one of these evils by remaining under the management of Aunt Katy. Then, too, I thought, since I had endured much in this line on Lloyd's plantation, I could endure as much elsewhere, and especially at Baltimore; for I had something of the feeling about that city which is expressed in the saying, that being "hanged in England, is better than dying a natural death in Ireland."

I had the strongest desire to see Baltimore. My cousin Tom—a boy two or three years older than I—had been there, and though not fluent (he stuttered immoderately) in speech, he had inspired me with that desire, by his eloquent description of the place. Tom was, sometimes, Capt. Auld's cabin boy; and when he came from Baltimore, he was always a sort of hero amongst us, at least till his Baltimore trip was forgotten. I could never tell him of anything, or point out anything that struck me as beautiful or powerful, but that he had seen something in Baltimore far surpassing it. Even the great house itself, with all its pictures within, and pillars without, he had the hardihood to say "was nothing to Baltimore." He bought a trumpet (worth six pence) and brought it home; told what he had seen in the windows of stores; that he had heard shooting crackers, and seen soldiers; that he had seen a steamboat; that there were ships in Baltimore that could carry four such sloops as the "Sally Lloyd." He said a great deal about the market house; he spoke of the bells ringing; and of many other things which roused my curiosity very much; and, indeed, which heightened my hopes of happiness in my new home.

We sailed out of Miles river for Baltimore early on a Saturday morning. I remember only the day of the week; for, at that time, I had no knowledge of the days of the month, nor, indeed, of the months of the year. On setting sail, I walked aft, and gave to Col. Lloyd's plantation what I hoped would be the last look I should ever give to it, or to any place like it. My strong aversion to the great farm, was not owing to my own personal suffering, but the daily suffering of others, and to the certainty that I must, sooner or later, be placed under the barbarous rule of an overseer, such as the accomplished Gore, or the brutal and drunken Plummer. After taking this last view, I quitted the quarter deck, made my way to the bow of the sloop, and spent the remainder of the day in looking ahead; interesting myself in what was in the distance, rather than what was near by or behind. The vessels, sweeping along the bay, were very interesting objects. The broad bay opened like a shoreless ocean on my boyish vision, filling me with wonder and admiration.

Late in the afternoon, we reached Annapolis, the capital of the state, stopping there not long enough to admit of my going ashore. It was the first large town I had ever seen; and though it was inferior to many a factory village in New England, my feelings, on seeing it, were excited to a pitch very little below that reached by travelers at the first view of Rome. The dome of the state house was especially imposing, and surpassed in grandeur the appearance of the great house. The great world was opening upon me very rapidly, and I was eagerly acquaint- ing myself with its multifarious lessons.

We arrived in Baltimore on Sunday morning, and landed at Smith's wharf, not far from Bowly's wharf. We had on board the sloop a large flock of sheep, for the Baltimore market; and, after assisting in driving them to the slaughter house of Mr. Curtis, on Loudon Slater's Hill, I was speedily conducted by Rich—one of the hands belonging to the sloop—to my new home in Alliciana street, near Gardiner's shipyard, on Fell's Point. Mr. and Mrs. Hugh Auld, my new mistress and master, were both at home, and met me at the door with their rosy cheeked little son, Thomas, to take care of whom was to constitute my future occupation.

In fact, it was to "little Tommy," rather than to his parents, that old master made a present of me; and though there was no legal form or arrangement entered into, I have no doubt that Mr. and Mrs. Auld felt that, in due time, I should be the legal property of their bright-eyed and beloved boy, Tommy. I was struck with the appearance, especially, of my new mistress. Her face was lighted with the kindliest emotions; and the reflex influence of her countenance, as well as the tenderness with which she seemed to regard me, while asking me sundry little questions, greatly delighted me, and lit up, to my fancy, the pathway of my future. Miss Lucretia was kind; but my new mistress, "Miss Sophy," surpassed her in kindness of manner. Little Thomas was affectionately told by his mother, that "there was his Freddy," and that "Freddy would take care of him;" and I was told to "be kind to little Tommy"—an injunction I scarcely needed, for I had already fallen in love with the dear boy; and with these little ceremonies I was initiated into my new home, and entered upon my peculiar duties, with not a cloud above the horizon.

I may say here, that I regard my removal from Col. Lloyd's plantation as one of the most interesting and fortunate events of my life. Viewing it in the light of human likelihoods, it is quite probable that, but for the mere circumstance of being thus removed before the rigors of slavery had fastened upon me; before my young spirit had been crushed under the iron control of the slave-driver, instead of being, today, a FREEMAN, I might have been wearing the galling chains of slavery. I have sometimes felt, however, that there was something more intelligent than chance, and something more certain than luck, to be seen in the circumstance. If I have made any progress in knowledge; if I have cherished any honorable aspirations, or have, in any manner, worthily discharged the duties of a member of an oppressed people; this little circumstance must be allowed its due weight in giving my life that direction. I have ever regarded it as the first plain manifestation of that Divinity that shapes our ends, Rough hew them as we will.

I was not the only boy on the plantation that might have been sent to live in Baltimore. There was a wide margin from which to select. There were boys younger, boys older, and boys of the same age, belonging to my old master some at his own house, and some at his farm — but the high privilege fell to me.

10

Life in Baltimore

Once in Baltimore, with hard brick pavements under my feet, which almost raised blisters, by their very heat, for it was in the height of summer; walled in on all sides by towering brick buildings; with troops of hostile boys ready to pounce upon me at every street corner; with new and strange objects glaring upon me at every step, and with startling sounds reaching my ears from all directions, I for a time thought that, after all, the home plantation was a more desirable place of residence than my home on Alliciana street, in Baltimore. My country eyes and ears were confused and bewildered here; but the boys were my chief trouble. They chased me, and called me "Eastern Shore man," till really I almost wished myself back on the Eastern Shore. I had to undergo a sort of moral acclimation, and when that was over, I did much better.

My new mistress happily proved to be all she seemed to be, when, with her husband, she met me at the door, with a most beaming, benignant countenance. She was, naturally, of an excellent disposition, kind, gentle and cheerful. The supercilious contempt for the rights and feelings of the slave, and the petulance and bad humor which generally characterize slaveholding ladies, were all quite absent from kind "Miss" Sophia's manner and bearing toward me. She had, in truth, never been a slaveholder, but had—a thing quite unusual in the south—depended almost entirely upon her own industry for a living. To this fact the dear lady, no doubt, owed the excellent preservation of her natural goodness of heart, for slavery can change a saint into a sinner, and an angel into a demon.

I hardly knew how to behave toward "Miss Sophia," as I used to call Mrs. Hugh Auld. I had been treated as a pig on the plantation; I was treated as a child now. I could not even approach her as I had formerly approached Mrs. Thomas Auld. How could I hang down my head, and speak with bated breath, when there was no pride to scorn me, no coldness to repel me, and no hatred to inspire me with fear? I therefore soon learned to regard her as something more akin to a mother, than a slaveholding mistress. The crouching servility of a slave, usually so acceptable a quality to the haughty slaveholder, was not understood nor desired by this gentle woman. So far from deeming it impudent in a slave to look her straight in the face, as some slaveholding ladies do, she seemed ever to say, "look up, child; don't be afraid; see, I am full of kindness and good will toward you."

The hands belonging to Col. Lloyd's sloop, esteemed it a great privilege to be the bearers of parcels or messages to my new mistress; for whenever they came, they were sure of a most kind and pleasant reception. If little Thomas was her son, and her most dearly beloved child, she, for a time, at least, made me something like his half-brother in her affections. If dear Tommy was exalted to a place on his mother's knee, "Feddy" was honored by a place at his mother's side. Nor did he lack the caressing strokes of her gentle hand, to convince him that, though motherless, he was not friendless. Mrs. Auld was not only a kind-hearted woman, but she was remarkably pious; frequent in her attendance of public worship, much given to reading the bible, and to chanting hymns of praise, when alone. Mr. Hugh Auld was altogether a different character. He cared very little about religion, knew more of the world, and was more of the world, than his wife. He set out, doubtless to be—as the world goes —a respectable man, and to get on by becoming a successful ship builder, in that city of ship building. This was his ambition, and it fully occupied him. I was, of course, of very little consequence to him, compared with what I was to good Mrs. Auld; and, when he smiled upon me, as he sometimes did, the smile was borrowed from his lovely wife, and, like all borrowed light, was transient, and vanished with the source whence it was derived.

While I must characterize Master Hugh as being a very sour man, and of forbidding appearance, it is due to him to acknowledge, that he was never very cruel to me, according to the notion of cruelty in Maryland. The first year or two which I spent in his house, he left me almost exclusively to the management of his wife. She was my law-giver. In hands so tender as hers, and in the absence of the cruelties of the plantation, I became, both physically and mentally, much more sensitive to good and ill treatment; and, perhaps, suffered more from a frown from my mistress, than I formerly did from a cuff at the hands of Aunt Katy. Instead of the cold, damp floor of my old master's kitchen, I found myself on carpets; for the corn bag in winter, I now had a good straw bed, well furnished with covers; for the coarse cornmeal in the morning, I now had good bread, and mush occasionally; for my poor tow-lien shirt, reaching to my knees, I had good, clean clothes. I was really well off.

My employment was to run errands, and to take care of Tommy; to prevent his getting in the way of carriages, and to keep him out of harm's way generally. Tommy, and I, and his mother, got on swimmingly together, for a time. I say for a time, because the fatal poison of irresponsible power, and the natural influence of slavery customs, were not long in making a suitable impression on the gentle and loving disposition of my excellent mistress. At first, Mrs. Auld evidently regarded me simply as a child, like any other child; she had not come to regard me as property. This latter thought was a thing of conventional growth. The first was natural and spontaneous. A noble nature, like hers, could not, instantly, be wholly perverted; and it took several years to change the natural sweetness of her temper into fretful bitterness. In her worst estate, however, there were, during the first seven years I lived with her, occasional returns of her former kindly disposition.

The frequent hearing of my mistress reading the bible, for she often read aloud when her husband was absent, soon awakened my curiosity in respect to this mystery of reading, and roused in me the desire to learn. Having no fear of my kind mistress before my eyes, (she had then given me no reason to fear,) I frankly asked her to teach me to read; and, without hesitation, the dear woman began the task, and very soon, by her assistance, I was master of the alphabet, and could spell words of three or four letters. My mistress seemed almost as proud of my progress, as if I had been her own child; and, supposing that her husband would be as well pleased, she made no secret of what she was doing for me. Indeed, she exultingly told him of the aptness of her pupil, of her intention to persevere in teaching me, and of the duty which she felt it to teach me, at least to read the bible. Here arose the first cloud over my Baltimore prospects, the precursor of drenching rains and chilling blasts.

Master Hugh was amazed at the simplicity of his spouse, and, probably for the first time, he unfolded to her the true philosophy of slavery, and the peculiar rules necessary to be observed by masters and mistresses, in the management of their human chattels. Mr. Auld promptly forbade continuance of her instruction; telling her, in the first place, that the thing itself was unlawful; that it was also unsafe, and could only lead to mischief. To use his own words, further, he said, "if you give a nigger an inch, he will take an ell;" "he should know nothing but the will of his master, and learn to obey it." "if you teach that nigger—speaking of myself—how to read the bible, there will be no keeping him;" "it would forever unfit him for the duties of a slave;" and "as to himself, learning would do him no good, but probably, a great deal of harm—making him disconsolate and unhappy." "If you learn him now to read, he'll want to know how to write; and, this accomplished, he'll be running away with himself."

Such was the tenor of Master Hugh's oracular exposition of the true philosophy of training a human chattel; and it must be confessed that he very clearly comprehended the nature and the requirements of the relation of master and slave. His discourse was the first decidedly anti-slavery lecture to which it had been my lot to listen. Mrs. Auld evidently felt the force of his remarks; and, like an obedient wife, began to shape her course in the direction indicated by her husband. The effect of his words, on me, was neither slight nor transitory. His iron sentences — cold and harsh — sunk deep into my heart, and stirred up not only my feelings into a sort of rebellion, but awakened within me a slumbering train of vital thought.

It was a new and special revelation, dispelling a painful mystery, against which my youthful understanding had struggled, and struggled in vain, to wit: the white man's power to perpetuate the enslavement of the black man. "Very well," thought I; "knowledge unfits a child to be a slave." I instinctively assented to the proposition; and from that moment I understood the direct pathway from slavery to freedom. This was just what I needed; and I got it at a time, and from a source, whence I least expected it. I was saddened at the thought of losing the assistance of my kind mistress; but the information, so instantly derived, to some extent compensated me for the loss I had sustained in this direction. Wise as Mr. Auld was, he evidently underrated my comprehension, and had little idea of the use to which I was capable of putting the impressive lesson he was giving to his wife. He wanted me to be a slave; I had already voted against that on the home plantation of Col. Lloyd. That which he most loved I most hated; and the very de- termination which he expressed to keep me in ignorance, only rendered me the more resolute in seeking intelligence. In learning to read, therefore, I am not sure that I do not owe quite as much to the opposition of my master, as to the kindly assistance of my amiable mistress. I acknowledge the benefit rendered me by the one, and by the other; believing, that but for my mistress, I might have grown up in ignorance.

I had resided but a short time in Baltimore, before I observed a marked difference in the manner of treating slaves, generally, from which I had witnessed in that isolated and out-of-the-way part of the country where I began life. A city slave is almost a free citizen, in Baltimore, compared with a slave on Col. Lloyd's plantation. He is much better fed and clothed, is less dejected in his appearance, and enjoys privileges altogether unknown to the whip-driven slave on the plantation. Slavery dislikes a dense population, in which there is a majority of non- slaveholders. The general sense of decency that must pervade such a population, does much to check and prevent those outbreaks of atrocious cruelty, and those dark crimes without a name, almost openly perpetrated on the plantation. He is a desperate slaveholder who will shock the humanity of his non- slaveholding neighbors, by the cries of the lacerated slaves; and very few in the city are willing to incur the odium of being cruel masters. I found, in Baltimore, that no man was more odious to the white, as well as to the colored people, than he, who had the reputation of starving his slaves. Work them, flog them, if need be, but don't starve them. These are, however, some painful exceptions to this rule. While it is quite true that most of the slaveholders in Baltimore feed and clothe their slaves well, there are others who keep up their country cruelties in the city.

An instance of this sort is furnished in the case of a family who lived directly opposite to our house, and were named Hamilton. Mrs. Hamilton owned two slaves. Their names were Henrietta and Mary. They had always been house slaves. One was aged about twenty-two, and the other about fourteen. They were a fragile couple by nature, and the treatment they received was enough to break down the constitution of a horse. Of all the dejected, emaciated, mangled and excoriated creatures I ever saw, those two girls—in the refined, church going and Christian city of Baltimore were the most deplorable. Of stone must that heart be made, that could look upon Henrietta and Mary, without being sickened to the core with sadness. Especially was Mary a heart-sickening object. Her head, neck and shoulders, were literally cut to pieces. I have frequently felt her head, and found it nearly covered over with festering sores, caused by the lash of her cruel mistress.

I do not know that her master ever whipped her, but I have often been an eye witness of the revolting and brutal inflictions by Mrs. Hamilton; and what lends a deeper shade to this woman's conduct, is the fact, that, almost in the very moments of her shocking outrages of humanity and decency, she would charm you by the sweetness of her voice and her seeming piety. She used to sit in a large rocking chair, near the middle of the room, with a heavy cowskin, such as I have elsewhere described; and I speak within the truth when I say, that these girls seldom passed that chair, during the day, without a blow from that cowskin, either upon their bare arms, or upon their shoulders. As they passed her, she would draw her cowskin and give them a blow, saying, "move faster, you black jip!" and, again, "take that, you black jip!" continuing, "if you don't move faster, I will give you more." Then the lady would go on, singing her sweet hymns, as though her righteous soul were sighing for the holy realms of paradise.

Added to the cruel lashings to which these poor slave-girls were subjected—enough in themselves to crush the spirit of men—they were, really, kept nearly half starved; they seldom knew what it was to eat a full meal, except when they got it in the kitchens of neighbors, less mean and stingy than the psalm-singing Mrs. Hamilton. I have seen poor Mary contending for the offal, with the pigs in the street. So much was the poor girl pinched, kicked, cut and pecked to pieces, that the boys in the street knew her only by the name of "pecked," a name derived from the scars and blotches on her neck, head and shoulders.

It is some relief to this picture of slavery in Baltimore, to say—what is but the simple truth—that Mrs. Hamilton's treatment of her slaves was generally condemned, as disgraceful and shocking; but while I say this, it must also be remembered, that the very parties who censured the cruelty of Mrs. Hamilton, would have condemned and promptly punished any attempt to interfere with Mrs. Hamilton's right to cut and slash her slaves to pieces. There must be no force between the slave and the slaveholder, to restrain the power of the one, and protect the weakness of the other; and the cruelty of Mrs. Hamilton is as justly chargeable to the upholders of the slave system, as drunkenness is chargeable on those who, by precept and example, or by indifference, uphold the drinking system.

11

"A Change Came O'er the Spirit of My Dream"

I lived in the family of Master Hugh, at Baltimore, seven years, during which time—as the almanac makers say of the weather—my condition was variable. The most interesting feature of my history here, was my learning to read and write, under somewhat marked disadvantages. In attaining this knowledge, I was compelled to resort to indirections by no means congenial to my nature, and which were really humiliating to me. My mistress—who, as the reader has already seen, had begun to teach me was suddenly checked in her benevolent design, by the strong advice of her husband. In faithful compliance with this advice, the good lady had not only ceased to instruct me, herself, but had set her face as a flint against my learning to read by any means. It is due, however, to my mistress to say, that she did not adopt this course in all its stringency at the first. She either thought it unnecessary, or she lacked the depravity indispensable to shutting me up in mental darkness. It was, at least, necessary for her to have some training, and some hardening, in the exercise of the slaveholder's prerogative, to make her equal to forgetting my human nature and character, and to treating me as a thing destitute of a moral or an intellectual nature.

Mrs. Auld—my mistress—was, as I have said, a most kind and tender-hearted woman; and, in the humanity of her heart, and the simplicity of her mind, she set out, when I first went to live with her, to treat me as she supposed one human being ought to treat another.

It is easy to see, that, in entering upon the duties of a slave-holder, some little experience is needed. Nature has done almost nothing to prepare men and women to be either slaves or slaveholders. Nothing but rigid training, long persisted in, can perfect the character of the one or the other. One cannot easily forget to love freedom; and it is as hard to cease to respect that natural love in our fellow creatures. On entering upon the career of a slaveholding mistress, Mrs. Auld was singularly deficient; nature, which fits nobody for such an office, had done less for her than any lady I had known. It was no easy matter to induce her to think and to feel that the curly-headed boy, who stood by her side, and even leaned on her lap; who was loved by little Tommy, and who loved little Tommy in turn; sustained to her only the relation of a chattel. I was more than that, and she felt me to be more than that. I could talk and sing; I could laugh and weep; I could reason and remember; I could love and hate. I was human, and she, dear lady, knew and felt me to be so. How could she, then, treat me as a brute, without a mighty struggle with all the noble powers of her own soul. That struggle came, and the will and power of the husband was victorious. Her noble soul was overthrown; but, he that overthrew it did not, himself, escape the consequences. He, not less than the other parties, was injured in his domestic peace by the fall.

When I went into their family, it was the abode of happiness and contentment. The mistress of the house was a model of affection and tenderness. Her fervent piety and watchful uprightness made it impossible to see her without thinking and feeling—"that woman is a Christian." There was no sorrow nor suffering for which she had not a tear, and there was no innocent joy for which she did not a smile. She had bread for the hungry, clothes for the naked, and comfort for every mourner that came within her reach. Slavery soon proved its ability to divest her of these excellent qualities, and her home of its early happiness. Conscience cannot stand much violence. Once thoroughly broken down, who is he that can repair the damage? It may be broken toward the slave, on Sunday, and toward the master on Monday. It cannot endure such shocks. It must stand entire, or it does not stand at all. If my condition waxed bad, that of the family waxed not better.

The first step, in the wrong direction, was the violence done to nature and to conscience, in arresting the benevolence that would have enlightened my young mind. In ceasing to instruct me, she must begin to justify herself to herself; and, once consenting to take sides in such a debate, she was riveted to her position. One needs very little knowledge of moral philosophy, to see where my mistress now landed. She finally became even more violent in her opposition to my learning to read, than was her husband himself. She was not satisfied with simply doing as well as her husband had commanded her, but seemed resolved to better his instruction. Nothing appeared to make my poor mistress—after her turning toward the downward path—more angry, than seeing me, seated in some nook or corner, quietly reading a book or a newspaper. I have had her rush at me, with the utmost fury, and snatch from my hand such newspaper or book, with something of the wrath and consternation which a traitor might be supposed to feel on being discovered in a plot by some dangerous spy.

Mrs. Auld was an apt woman, and the advice of her husband, and her own experience, soon demonstrated, to her entire satisfaction, that education and slavery are incompatible with each other. When this conviction was thoroughly established, I was most narrowly watched in all my movements. If I remained in a separate room from the family for any considerable length of time, I was sure to be suspected of having a book, and was at once called upon to give an account of myself. All this, however, was entirely too late. The first, and never to be retraced, step had been taken. In teaching me the alphabet, in the days of her simplicity and kindness, my mistress had given me the "inch," and now, no ordinary precaution could prevent me from taking the "ell."

Seized with a determination to learn to read, at any cost, I hit upon many expedients to accomplish the desired end. The plea which I mainly adopted, and the one by which I was most successful, was that of using my young white playmates, with whom I met in the streets as teachers. I used to carry, almost constantly, a copy of Webster's spelling book in my pocket; and, when sent of errands, or when play time was allowed me, I would step, with my young friends, aside, and take a lesson in spelling. I generally paid my tuition fee to the boys, with bread, which I also carried in my pocket. For a single biscuit, any of my hungry little comrades would give me a lesson more valuable to me than bread.

Not everyone, however, demanded this consideration, for there were those who took pleasure in teaching me, whenever I had a chance to be taught by them. I am strongly tempted to give the names of two or three of those little boys, as a slight testimonial of the gratitude and affection I bear them, but prudence forbids; not that it would injure me, but it might, possibly, embarrass them; for it is almost an unpardonable offense to do anything, directly or indirectly, to promote a slave's freedom, in a slave state. It is enough to say, of my warm-hearted little play fellows, that they lived on Philpot street, very near Durgin & Bailey's shipyard.

Although slavery was a delicate subject, and very cautiously talked about among grown up people in Maryland, I frequently talked about it—and that very freely—with the white boys. I would, sometimes, say to them, while seated on a curb stone or a cellar door, "I wish I could be free, as you will be when you get to be men." "You will be free, you know, as soon as you are twenty-one, and can go where you like, but I am a slave for life. Have I not as good a right to be free as you have?" Words like these, I observed, always troubled them; and I had no small satisfaction in wringing from the boys, occasionally, that fresh and bitter condemnation of slavery, that springs from nature, unseared and unperverted. Of all consciences let me have those to deal with which have not been bewildered by the cares of life. I do not remember ever to have met with a boy, while I was in slavery, who defended the slave system; but I have often had boys to console me, with the hope that something would yet occur, by which I might be made free. Over and over again, they have told me, that "they believed I had as good a right to be free as they had;" and that "they did not believe God ever made anyone to be a slave." The reader will easily see, that such little conversations with my play fellows, had no tendency to weaken my love of liberty, nor to render me contented with my condition as a slave.

When I was about thirteen years old, and had succeeded in learning to read, every increase of knowledge, especially respecting the FREE STATES, added something to the almost in- tolerable burden of the thought—I AM A SLAVE FOR LIFE. To my bondage I saw no end. It was a terrible reality, and I shall never be able to tell how sadly that thought chafed my young spirit. Fortunately, or unfortunately, about this time in my life, I had made enough money to buy what was then a very popular school book: the Columbian Orator. I bought this addition to my library, of Mr. Knight, on Thames street, Fell's Point, Baltimore, and paid him fifty cents for it. I was first led to buy this book, by hearing some little boys say they were going to learn some little pieces out of it for the Exhibition. This volume was, indeed, a rich treasure, and every opportunity afforded me, for a time, was spent in diligently perusing it.

Among much other interesting matter, that which I had perused and reperused with unflagging satisfaction, was a short dialogue between a master and his slave. The slave is represented as having been recaptured, in a second attempt to run away; and the master opens the dialogue with an upbraiding speech, charging the slave with ingratitude, and demanding to know what he has to say in his own defense. Thus upbraided, and thus called upon to reply, the slave rejoins, that he knows how little anything that he can say will avail, seeing that he is completely in the hands of his owner; and with noble resolution, calmly says, "I submit to my fate." Touched by the slave's answer, the master insists upon his further speaking, and recapitulates the many acts of kindness which he has performed toward the slave, and tells him he is permitted to speak for himself. Thus invited to the debate, the quondam slave made a spirited defense of himself, and thereafter the whole argument, for and against slavery, was brought out. The master was vanquished at every turn in the argument; and seeing himself to be thus vanquished, he generously and meekly emancipates the slave, with his best wishes for his prosperity.

It is scarcely necessary to say, that a dialogue, with such an origin, and such an ending—read when the fact of my being a slave was a constant burden of grief—powerfully affected me; and I could not help feeling that the day might come, when the well-directed answers made by the slave to the master, in this instance, would find their counterpart in myself.

This, however, was not all the fanaticism which I found in this Columbian Orator. I met there one of Sheridan's mighty speeches, on the subject of Catholic Emancipation, Lord Chatham's speech on the American war, and speeches by the great William Pitt and by Fox. These were all choice documents to me, and I read them, over and over again, with an interest that was ever increasing, because it was ever gaining in intelligence; for the more I read them, the better I understood them. The reading of these speeches added much to my limited stock of language, and enabled me to give tongue to many interesting thoughts, which had frequently flashed through my soul, and died away for want of utterance. From the speeches of Sheridan, I got a bold and powerful denunciation of oppression, and a most brilliant vindication of the rights of man. Here was, indeed, a noble acquisition. If I ever wavered under the consideration, that the Almighty, in some way, ordained slavery, and willed my enslavement for his own glory, I wavered no longer. I had now penetrated the secret of all slavery and oppression, and had ascertained their true foundation to be in the pride, the power and the avarice of man. The dialogue and the speeches were all redolent of the principles of liberty, and poured floods of light on the nature and character of slavery. With a book of this kind in my hand, my own human nature, and the facts of my experience, to help me, I was equal to a contest with the religious advocates of slavery, whether among the whites or among the colored people, for blindness, in this matter, is not confined to the former.

I have met many religious colored people, at the south, who are under the delusion that God requires them to submit to slavery, and to wear their chains with meekness and humility. I could entertain no such nonsense as this;

and I almost lost my patience when I found any colored man weak enough to believe such stuff. Nevertheless, the increase of knowledge was attended with bitter, as well as sweet results. The more I read, the more I was led to abhor and detest slavery, and my enslavers. "Slaveholders," thought I, "are only a band of successful robbers, who left their homes and went into Africa for the purpose of stealing and reducing my people to slavery." I loathed them as the meanest and the most wicked of men. As I read, behold! the very discontent so graphically predicted by Master Hugh, had already come upon me. I was no longer the light-hearted, gleesome boy, full of mirth and play, as when I landed first at Baltimore. Knowledge had come; light had penetrated the moral dungeon where I dwelt; and, behold! there lay the bloody whip, for my back, and here was the iron chain; and my good, kind master, he was the author of my situation. The revelation haunted me, stung me, and made me gloomy and miserable. As I writhed under the sting and torment of this knowledge, I almost envied my fellow slaves their stupid contentment. This knowledge opened my eyes to the horrible pit, and revealed the teeth of the frightful dragon that was ready to pounce upon me, but it opened no way for my escape.

I have often wished myself a beast, or a bird—anything, rather than a slave. I was wretched and gloomy, beyond my ability to describe. I was too thoughtful to be happy. It was this everlasting thinking which distressed and tormented me; and yet there was no getting rid of the subject of my thoughts. All nature was redolent of it. Once awakened by the silver trump of knowledge, my spirit was roused to eternal wakefulness. Liberty! the inestimable birthright of every man, had, for me, converted every object into an asserter of this great right.

It was heard in every sound, and beheld in every object. It was ever present, to torment me with a sense of my wretched condition. The more beautiful and charming were the smiles of nature, the more horrible and desolate was my condition. I saw nothing without seeing it, and I heard nothing without hearing it. I do not exaggerate, when I say, that it looked from every star, smiled in every calm, breathed in every wind, and moved in every storm.

I have no doubt that my state of mind had something to do with the change in the treatment adopted, by my once kind mistress toward me. I can easily believe, that my leaden, downcast, and discontented look, was very offensive to her. Poor lady! She did not know my trouble, and I dared not tell her. Could I have freely made her acquainted with the real state of my mind, and given her the reasons therefore, it might have been well for both of us. Her abuse of me fell upon me like the blows of the false prophet upon his ass; she did not know that an angel stood in the way; and—such is the relation of master and slave I could not tell her. Nature had made us friends; slavery made us enemies. My interests were in a direction opposite to hers, and we both had our private thoughts and plans. She aimed to keep me ignorant; and I resolved to know, although knowledge only increased my discontent. My feelings were not the result of any marked cruelty in the treatment I received; they sprung from the consideration of my being a slave at all. It was slavery—not its mere incidents—that I hated. I had been cheated. I saw through the attempt to keep me in ignorance; I saw that slave-holders would have gladly made me believe that they were merely acting under the authority of God, in making a slave of me, and in making slaves of others; and I treated them as robbers and deceivers. The feeding and clothing me well, could not atone for taking my liberty from me. The smiles of my mistress could not remove the deep sorrow that dwelt in my young bosom. Indeed, these, in time, came only to deepen my sorrow. She had changed; and the reader will see that I had changed, too. We were both victims to the same overshadowing evil—she, as mistress, I, as slave. I will not censure her harshly; she cannot censure me, for she knows I speak but the truth, and have acted in my opposition to slavery, just as she herself would have acted, in a reverse of circumstances.

12

Religious Nature Awakened

While in the painful state of mind described in the foregoing chapter, almost regretting my very existence, because doomed to a life of bondage, so goaded and so wretched, at times, that I was even tempted to destroy my own life, I was keenly sensitive and eager to know any, and every thing that transpired, having any relation to the subject of slavery. I was all ears, all eyes, whenever the words slave, slavery, dropped from the lips of any white person, and the occasions were not unfrequent when these words became leading ones, in high, social debate, at our house. Every little while, I could hear Master Hugh, or some of his company, speaking with much warmth and excitement about "abolitionists." Of who or what these were, I was totally ignorant. I found, however, that whatever they might be, they were most cordially hated and soundly abused by slaveholders, of every grade. I very soon discovered, too, that slavery was, in some sort, under consideration, whenever the abolitionists were alluded to. This made the term a very interesting one to me. If a slave, for instance, had made good his escape from slavery, it was generally alleged, that he had been persuaded and assisted by the abolitionists. If, also, a slave killed his master—as was sometimes the case—or struck down his overseer, or set fire to his master's dwelling, or committed any violence or crime, out of the common way, it was certain to be said, that such a crime was the legitimate fruits of the abolition movement. Hearing such charges often repeated, I, naturally enough, received the impression that abolition—whatever else it might be—could not be unfriendly to the slave, nor very friendly to the slaveholder. I therefore set about finding out, if possible, who and what the abolitionists were, and why they were so obnoxious to the slaveholders.

The dictionary afforded me very little help. It taught me that abolition was the "act of abolishing;" but it left me in ignorance at the very point where I most wanted information—and that was, as to the thing to be abolished. A city newspaper, the Baltimore American, gave me the incendiary information denied me by the dictionary. In its columns I found, that, on a certain day, a vast number of petitions and memorials had been presented to congress, praying for the abolition of slavery in the District of Columbia, and for the abolition of the slave trade between the states of the Union. This was enough. The vindictive bitterness, the marked caution, the studied reverse, and the cumbrous ambiguity, practiced by our white folks, when alluding to this subject, was now fully explained. Ever, after that, when I heard the words "abolition," or "abolition movement," mentioned, I felt the matter one of a personal concern; and I drew near to listen, when I could do so, without seeming too solicitous and prying. There was HOPE in those words.

Soon too, I could see some terrible denunciation of slavery, in our papers—copied from abolition papers at the north—and the injustice of such denunciation commented on. These I read with avidity. I had a deep satisfaction in the thought, that the rascality of slaveholders was not concealed from the eyes of the world, and that I was not alone in abhorring the cruelty and brutality of slavery. A still deeper train of thought was stirred. I saw that there was fear, as well as rage, in the manner of speaking of the abolitionists. The latter, therefore, I was compelled to regard as having some power in the country; and I felt that they might, possibly, succeed in their designs.

When I met with a slave to whom I deemed it safe to talk on the subject, I would impart to him so much of the mystery as I had been able to penetrate. Thus, the light of this grand movement broke in upon my mind, by degrees; and I must say, that, ignorant as I then was of the philosophy of that movement, I believe in it from the first—and I believed in it, partly, because I saw that it alarmed the consciences of slaveholders. The insurrection of Nathaniel Turner had been quelled, but the alarm and terror had not subsided. The cholera was on its way, and the thought was present, that God was angry with the white people because of their slaveholding wickedness, and, therefore, his judgments were abroad in the land. It was impossible for me not to hope much from the abolition movement, when I saw it supported by the Almighty, and armed with DEATH!

Previous to my contemplation of the anti-slavery movement, and its probable results, my mind had been seriously awakened to the subject of religion. I was not more than thirteen years old, when I felt the need of God, as a father and protector. My religious nature was awakened by the preaching of a white Methodist minister, named Hanson. He thought that all men, great and small, bond and free, were sinners in the sight of God; that they were, by nature, rebels against His government; and that they must repent of their sins, and be reconciled to God, through Christ. I cannot say that I had a very distinct notion of what was required of me; but one thing I knew very well—I was wretched, and had no means of making myself otherwise. Moreover, I knew that I could pray for light. I consulted a good colored man, named Charles Johnson; and, in tones of holy affection, he told me to pray, and what to pray for. I was, for weeks, a poor, brokenhearted mourner, traveling through the darkness and misery of doubts and fears. I finally found that change of heart which comes by "casting all one's care" upon God, and by having faith in Jesus Christ, as the Redeemer, Friend, and Savior of those who diligently seek Him.

After this, I saw the world in a new light. I seemed to live in a new world, surrounded by new objects, and to be animated by new hopes and desires. I loved all mankind

—slaveholders not excepted; though I abhorred slavery more than ever. The desire for knowledge increased, and especially did I want a thorough acquaintance with the contents of the bible. I have gathered scattered pages from this holy book, from the filthy street gutters of Baltimore, and washed and dried them, that in the moments of my leisure, I might get a word or two of wisdom from them.

While thus religiously seeking knowledge, I became acquainted with a good old colored man, named Lawson. A more devout man than he, I never saw. This man not only prayed three time a day. His life was a life of prayer, and his words (when he spoke to his friends,) were about a better world. Uncle Lawson lived near Master Hugh's house; and, becoming deeply attached to the old man, I went often with him to prayer-meeting, and spent much of my leisure time with him on Sunday. The old man could read a little, and I was a great help to him, in making out the hard words, for I was a better reader than he. I could teach him "the letter," but he could teach me "the spirit;" and high, refreshing times we had together, in singing, praying and glorifying God. These meetings with Uncle Lawson went on for a long time, without the knowledge of Master Hugh or my mistress. Both knew, however, that I had become religious, and they seemed to respect my conscientious piety.

Uncle Lawson, he was my spiritual father; and I loved him intensely, and was at his house every chance I got. This pleasure was not long allowed me. Master Hugh became averse to my going to Father Lawson's, and threatened to whip me if I ever went there again. I now felt myself persecuted by a wicked man; and I would go to Father Lawson's, notwithstanding the threat. The good old man had told me, that the "Lord had a great work for me to do;" and I must prepare to do it; and that he had been shown that I must preach the gospel. His words made a deep impression on my mind, and I verily felt that some such work was before me, though I could not see how I should ever engage in its performance.

"The good Lord," he said, "would bring it to pass in his own good time," and that I must go on reading and studying the scriptures. The advice and the suggestions of Uncle Lawson, were not without their influence upon my character and destiny. He threw my thoughts into a channel from which they have never entirely diverged. He fanned my already intense love of knowledge into a flame, by assuring me that I was to be a useful man in the world. When I would say to him, "How can these things be and what can I do?" his simple reply was, "Trust in the Lord." When I told him that "I was a slave, and a slave FOR LIFE," he said, "the Lord can make you free, my dear. All things are possible with him, only have faith in God." "Ask, and it shall be given." "If you want liberty," said the good old man, "ask the Lord for it, in faith, AND HE WILL GIVE IT TO YOU."

Thus assured, and cheered on, under the inspiration of hope, I worked and prayed with a light heart, believing that my life was under the guidance of a wisdom higher than my own. With all other blessings sought at the mercy seat, I always prayed that God would, of His great mercy, and in His own good time, deliver me from my bondage.

I went, one day, on the wharf of Mr. Waters; and seeing two Irishmen unloading a large scow of stone, or ballast I went on board, unasked, and helped them. When we had finished the work, one of the men came to me, aside, and asked me a number of questions, and among them, if I were a slave. I told him "I was a slave, and a slave for life." The good Irishman gave his shoulders a shrug, and seemed deeply affected by the statement. He said, "it was a pity so fine a little fellow as myself should be a slave for life." They both had much to say about the matter, and expressed the deepest sympathy with me, and the most decided hatred of slavery. They went so far as to tell me that I ought to run away, and go to the north; that I should find friends there, and that I would be as free as anybody. I, however, pretended not to be interested in what they said, for I feared they might be treacherous. White men have been known to encourage slaves to escape, and then—to get the reward—they have kidnapped them, and returned them to their masters. And while I mainly inclined to the notion that these men were honest and meant me no ill, I feared it might be otherwise.

I nevertheless remembered their words and their ad- vice, and looked forward to an escape to the north, as a possible means of gaining the liberty for which my heart panted. It was not my enslavement, at the then present time, that most affected me; the being a slave for life, was the saddest thought. I was too young to think of running away immediately; besides, I wished to learn how to write, before going, as I might have occasion to write my own pass. I now not only had the hope of freedom, but a foreshadowing of the means by which I might, some day, gain that inestimable boon. Meanwhile, I resolved to add to my educational attainments the art of writing.

After this manner I began to learn to write: I was much in the shipyard—Master Hugh's, and that of Durgan & Bailey—and I observed that the carpenters, after hewing and getting a piece of timber ready for use, wrote on it the initials of the name of that part of the ship for which it was intended. When, for instance, a piece of timber was ready for the starboard side, it was marked with a capital "S." A piece for the larboard side was marked "L;" larboard forward, "L. F.;" larboard aft, was marked "L. A.;" starboard aft, "S. A.;" and starboard forward "S. F." I soon learned these letters, and for what they were placed on the timbers.

My work was now, to keep fire under the steam box, and to watch the shipyard while the carpenters had gone to dinner. This interval gave me a fine opportunity for copying the letters named. I soon astonished myself with the ease with which I made the letters; and the thought was soon present, "if I can make four, I can make more." But having made these easily, when I met boys about Bethel church, or any of our playgrounds, I entered the lists with them in the art of writing, and would make the letters which I had been so fortunate as to learn, and ask them to "beat that if they could." With playmates for my teachers, fences and pavements for my copy books, and chalk for my pen and ink, I learned the art of writing. I, however, afterward adopted various methods of improving my hand. The most successful was copying the italics in Webster's spelling book, until I could make them all without looking on the book. By this time, my little "Master Tommy" had grown to be a big boy, and had written over a number of copy books, and brought them home. They had been shown to the neighbors, had elicited due praise, and were now laid carefully away. Spending my time between the shipyard and house, I was as often the lone keeper of the latter as of the former. When my mistress left me in charge of the house, I had a grand time; I got Master Tommy's copy books and a pen and ink, and, in the ample spaces between the lines, I wrote other lines, as nearly like his as possible.

The process was a tedious one, and I ran the risk of getting a flogging for marring the highly prized copy books of the oldest son. In addition to those opportunities, sleeping, as I did, in the kitchen loft—a room seldom visited by any of the family—I got a flour barrel up there, and a chair; and upon the head of that barrel I have written (or endeavored to write) copying from the bible and the Methodist hymn book, and other books which had accumulated on my hands, till late at night, and when all the family were in bed and asleep. I was supported in my endeavors by renewed advice, and by holy promises from the good Father Lawson, with whom I continued to meet, and pray, and read the scriptures. Although Master Hugh was aware of my going there, I must say, for his credit, that he never executed his threat to whip me, for having thus, innocently, employed my leisure time.

13

The Vicissitudes of Slave Life

I must now ask the reader to go with me a little back in point of time, in my humble story, and to notice another circumstance that entered into my slavery experience, and which, doubtless, has had a share in deepening my horror of slavery, and increasing my hostility toward those men and measures that practically uphold the slave system.

It has already been observed, that though I was, after my removal from Col. Lloyd's plantation, in form the slave of Master Hugh, I was, in fact, and in law, the slave of my old master, Capt. Anthony. Very well.

In a very short time after I went to Baltimore, my old master's youngest son, Richard, died; and, in three years and six months after his death, my old master himself died, leaving only his son, Andrew, and his daughter, Lucretia, to share his estate. The old man died while on a visit to his daughter, in Hillsborough, where Capt. Auld and Mrs. Lucretia now lived. The former, having given up the command of Col. Lloyd's sloop, was now keeping a store in that town.

Cut off, thus unexpectedly, Capt. Anthony died intestate; and his property must now be equally divided between his two children, Andrew and Lucretia.

The valuation and the division of slaves, among contending heirs, is an important incident in slave life. The character and tendencies of the heirs are generally well understood among the slaves who are to be divided, and all have their aversions and preferences. But neither their aversions nor their preferences avail them anything.

On the death of old master, I was immediately sent for, to be valued and divided with the other property. Personally, my concern was, mainly, about my possible removal from the home of Master Hugh, which, after that of my grandmother, was the most endeared to me. But, the whole thing, as a feature of slavery, shocked me. It furnished me a new insight into the unnatural power to which I was subjected. My detestation of slavery, already great, rose with this new conception of its enormity.

That was a sad day for me, a sad day for little Tommy, and a sad day for my dear Baltimore mistress and teacher, when I left for the Eastern Shore, to be valued and divided. We, all three, wept bitterly that day; for we might be parting, and we feared we were parting, forever. No one could tell among which pile of chattels I should be flung. Thus early, I got a foretaste of that painful uncertainty which slavery brings to the ordinary lot of mortals. Sickness, adversity and death may interfere with the plans and purposes of all; but the slave has the added danger of changing homes, changing hands, and of having separations unknown to other men. Then, too, there was the intensified degradation of the spectacle. What an assemblage! Men and women, young and old, married and single; moral and intellectual beings, in open contempt of their humanity, level at a blow with horses, sheep, horned cattle and swine! Horses and men—cattle and women—pigs and children—all holding the same rank in the scale of social existence; and all subjected to the same narrow inspection, to ascertain their value in gold and silver—the only standard of worth applied by slaveholders to slaves! How vividly, at that moment, did the brutalizing power of slavery flash before me! Personality swallowed up in the sordid idea of property! Manhood lost in chattelhood!

After the valuation, then came the division. This was an hour of high excitement and distressing anxiety. Our destiny was now to be fixed for life, and we had no more voice in the decision of the question, than the oxen and cows that stood chewing at the haymow. One word from the appraisers, against all preferences or prayers, was enough to sunder all the ties of friendship and affection, and even to separate husbands and wives, parents and children. We were all appalled before that power, which, to human seeming, could bless or blast us in a moment. Added to the dread of separation, most painful to the majority of the slaves, we all had a decided horror of the thought of falling into the hands of Master Andrew. He was distinguished for cruelty and intemperance.

Slaves generally dread to fall into the hands of drunken owners. Master Andrew was almost a confirmed sot, and had already, by his reckless mismanagement and profligate dissipation, wasted a large portion of old master's property. To fall into his hands, was, therefore, considered merely as the first step toward being sold away to the far south. He would spend his fortune in a few years, and his farms and slaves would be sold, we thought, at public outcry; and we should be hurried away to the cotton fields, and rice swamps, of the sunny south. This was the cause of deep consternation.

The people of the north, and free people generally, I think, have less attachment to the places where they are born and brought up, than have the slaves. Their freedom to go and come, to be here and there, as they list, prevents any extravagant attachment to any one particular place, in their case. On the other hand, the slave is a fixture; he has no choice, no goal, no destination; but is pegged down to a single spot, and must take root here, or nowhere. The idea of removal elsewhere, comes, generally, in the shape of a threat, and in punishment of crime. It is, therefore, attended with fear and dread. A slave seldom thinks of bettering his condition by being sold, and hence he looks upon separation from his native place, with none of the enthusiasm which animates the bosoms of young freemen, when they contemplate a life in the far west, or in some distant country where they intend to rise to wealth and distinction. Nor can those from whom they separate, give them up with that cheerfulness with which friends and relations yield each other up, when they feel that it is for the good of the departing one that he is removed from his native place. Then, too, there is correspondence, and there is, at least, the hope of reunion, because reunion is possible. But, with the slave, all these mitigating circumstances are wanting. There is no improvement in his condition probable,—no correspondence possible,—no reunion attainable. His going out into the world, is like a living man going into the tomb, who, with open eyes, sees himself buried out of sight and hearing of wife, children and friends of kindred tie.

In contemplating the likelihoods and possibilities of our circumstances, I probably suffered more than most of my fellow servants. I had known what it was to experience kind, and even tender treatment; they had known nothing of the sort. Life, to them, had been rough and thorny, as well as dark. They had—most of them—lived on my old master's farm in Tuckahoe, and had felt the reign of Mr. Plummer's rule. The overseer had written his character on the living parchment of most of their backs, and left them callous; my back (thanks to my early removal from the plantation to Baltimore) was yet tender. I had left a kind mistress at Baltimore, who was almost a mother to me. She was in tears when we parted, and the probabilities of ever seeing her again, trembling in the balance as they did, could not be viewed without alarm and agony. The thought of leaving that kind mistress forever, and, worse still, of being the slave of Andrew Anthony—a man who, but a few days before the division of the property, had, in my presence, seized my brother Perry by the throat, dashed him on the ground, and with the heel of his boot stamped him on the head, until the blood gushed from his nose and ears—was terrible! This fiendish proceeding had no better apology than the fact, that Perry had gone to play, when Master Andrew wanted him for some trifling service. This cruelty, too, was of a piece with his general character. After inflicting his heavy blows on my brother, on observing me looking at him with intense astonishment, he said, "That is the way I will serve you, one of these days;" meaning, no doubt, when I should come into his possession. This threat, the reader may well suppose, was not very tranquilizing to my feelings. I could see that he really thirsted to get hold of me. But I was there only for a few days. I had not received any orders, and had violated none, and there was, therefore, no excuse for flogging me.

At last, the anxiety and suspense were ended; and they ended, thanks to a kind Providence, in accordance with my wishes. I fell to the portion of Mrs. Lucretia—the dear lady who bound up my head, when the savage Aunt Katy was adding to my sufferings her bitterest maledictions.

Capt. Thomas Auld and Mrs. Lucretia at once decided on my return to Baltimore. They knew how sincerely and warmly Mrs. Hugh Auld was attached to me, and how delighted Mr. Hugh's son would be to have me back; and having no immediate use for one so young, they willingly let me off to Baltimore.

I need not stop here to narrate my joy on returning to Baltimore, nor that of little Tommy; nor the tearful joy of his mother; nor the evident satisfaction of Master Hugh. I was just one month absent from Baltimore, before the matter was decided; and the time really seemed full six months.

One trouble over, and on comes another. The slave's life is full of uncertainty. I had returned to Baltimore but a short time, when the tidings reached me, that my friend, Mrs. Lucretia, who was only second in my regard to Mrs. Hugh Auld, was dead, leaving her husband and only one child—a daughter, named Amanda.

Shortly after the death of Mrs. Lucretia, strange to say, Master Andrew died, leaving his wife and one child. Thus, the whole family of Anthonys was swept away; only two children remained. All this happened within five years of my leaving Col. Lloyd's.

No alteration took place in the condition of the slaves, in consequence of these deaths, yet I could not help feeling less secure, after the death of my friend, Mrs. Lucretia, than I had done during her life. While she lived, I felt that I had a strong friend to plead for me in any emergency. Ten years ago, while speaking of the state of things in our family, after the events just named, I used this language:

"Now all the property of my old master, slaves included, was in the hands of strangers—strangers who had nothing to do in accumulating it. Not a slave was left free. All remained slaves, from youngest to oldest. If any one thing in my experience, more than another, served to deepen my conviction of the infernal character of slavery, and to fill me with unutterable loathing of slaveholders, it was their base ingratitude to my poor old grandmother. She had served my old master faithfully from youth to old age. She had been the source of all his wealth; she had peopled his plantation with slaves; she had become a great-grandmother in his service. She had rocked him in infancy, attended him in childhood, served him through life, and at his death wiped from his icy brow the cold death-sweat, and closed his eyes forever. She was nevertheless left a slave—a slave for life—a slave in the hands of strangers; and in their hands she saw her children, her grandchildren, and her great-grandchildren, divided, like so many sheep, without being gratified with the small privilege of a single word, as to their or her own destiny. And, to cap the climax of their base ingratitude and fiendish barbarity, my grandmother, who was now very old, having outlived my old master and all his children, having seen the beginning and end of all of them, and her present owners finding she was of but little value, her frame already racked with the pains of old age, and complete helplessness fast stealing over her once active limbs, they took her to the woods, built her a little hut, put up a little mud-chimney, and then made her welcome to the privilege of supporting herself there in perfect loneliness; thus virtually turning her out to die! If my poor old grandmother now lives, she lives to suffer in utter loneliness; she lives to remember and mourn over the loss of children, the loss of grandchildren, and the loss of great-grandchildren. They are, in the language of the slave's poet, Whittier—

Gone, gone, sold and gone,
To the rice swamp dank and lone,
Where the slave-whip ceaseless swings,
Where the noisome insect stings,
Where the fever-demon strews
Poison with the falling dews,
Where the sickly sunbeams glare
Through the hot and misty air:—
Gone, gone, sold and gone
To the rice swamp dank and lone,
From Virginia hills and waters—
Woe is me, my stolen daughters!

The hearth is desolate. The children, the unconscious children, who once sang and danced in her presence, are gone. She gropes her way, in the darkness of age, for a drink of water. Instead of the voices of her children, she hears by day the moans of the dove, and by night the screams of the hideous owl. All is gloom. The grave is at the door. And now, when weighed down by the pains and aches of old age, when the head inclines to the feet, when the beginning and ending of human existence meet, and helpless infancy and painful old age combine together— at this time, this most needful time, the time for the exercise of that tenderness and affection which children only can exercise toward a declining parent—my poor old grandmother, the devoted mother of twelve children, is left all alone, in yonder little hut, before a few dim embers."

Two years after the death of Mrs. Lucretia, Master Thomas married his second wife. Her name was Rowena Hamilton, the eldest daughter of Mr. William Hamilton, a rich slaveholder on the Eastern Shore of Maryland, who lived about five miles from St. Michael's, the then place of my master's residence.

Not long after his marriage, Master Thomas had a misunderstanding with Master Hugh, and, as a means of punishing his brother, he ordered him to send me home. As the ground of misunderstanding will serve to illustrate the character of southern chivalry, and humanity, I will relate it.

Among the children of my Aunt Milly, was a daughter named Henny. When quite a child, Henny had fallen into the fire, and burnt her hands so bad that they were of very little use to her. Her fingers were drawn almost into the palms of her hands. She could make out to do something, but she was considered hardly worth the having—of little more value than a horse with a broken leg. This unprofitable piece of human property, ill shaped, and disfigured, Capt. Auld sent off to Baltimore, making his brother Hugh welcome to her services.

After giving poor Henny a fair trial, Master Hugh and his wife came to the conclusion, that they had no use for the crippled servant, and they sent her back to Master Thomas. Thus, the latter took as an act of ingratitude, on the part of his brother; and, as a mark of his displeasure, he required him to send me immediately to St. Michael's, saying, if he cannot keep "Hen," he shall not have "Fred."

Here was another shock to my nerves, another breaking up of my plans, and another severance of my religious and social alliances. I was now a big boy. I had become quite useful to several young colored men, who had made me their teacher. I had taught some of them to read, and was accustomed to spend many of my leisure hours with them. Our attachment was strong, and I greatly dreaded the separation. But regrets, especially in a slave, are unavailing. I was only a slave; my wishes were nothing, and my happiness was the sport of my masters.

My regrets at now leaving Baltimore, were not for the same reasons as when I before left that city, to be valued and handed over to my proper owner. My home was not now the pleasant place it had formerly been. A change had taken place, both in Master Hugh, and in his once pious and affectionate wife. The influence of brandy and bad company on him, and the influence of slavery and social isolation upon her, had wrought disastrously upon the characters of both. Thomas was no longer "little

Tommy," but was a big boy, and had learned to assume the airs of his class toward me. My condition, therefore, in the house of Master Hugh, was not, by any means, so comfortable as in former years. My attachments were now outside of our family. They were felt to those to whom I imparted instruction, and to those little white boys from whom I received instruction. There, too, was my dear old father, the pious Lawson, who was, in christian graces, the very counterpart of "Uncle Tom". The resemblance is so perfect, that he might have been the original of Mrs. Stowe's christian hero. The thought of leaving these dear friends, greatly troubled me, for I was going without the hope of ever returning to Baltimore again; the feud between Master Hugh and his brother being bitter and irreconcilable, or, at least, supposed to be so.

In addition to thoughts of friends from whom I was parting, as I supposed, forever, I had the grief of neglected chances of escape to brood over. I had put off running away, until now I was to be placed where the opportunities for escaping were much fewer than in a large city like Baltimore.

On my way from Baltimore to St. Michael's, down the Chesapeake bay, our sloop—the "Amanda"—was passed by the steamers plying between that city and Philadelphia, and I watched the course of those steamers, and, while going to St. Michael's, I formed a plan to escape from slavery; of which plan, and matters connected therewith the kind reader shall learn more hereafter.

14

Experience in St. Michael's

St. Michael's, the village in which was now my new home, compared favorably with villages in slave states, generally. There were a few comfortable dwellings in it, but the place, as a whole, wore a dull, slovenly, enterprise-forsaken aspect. The mass of the buildings were wood; they had never enjoyed the artificial adornment of paint, and time and storms had worn off the bright color of the wood, leaving them almost as black as buildings charred by a conflagration.

St. Michael's had, in former years, (previous to 1833, for that was the year I went to reside there,) enjoyed some reputation as a ship building community, but that business had almost entirely given place to oyster fishing, for the Baltimore and Philadelphia markets. Miles river was broad, and its oyster fishing grounds were extensive; and the fishermen were out, often, all day, and a part of the night, during autumn, winter and spring. This exposure was an excuse for carrying with them, in considerable quantities, spirituous liquors, the then supposed best antidote for cold. Each canoe was supplied with its jug of rum; and tippling, among this class of the citizens of St. Michael's, became general. This drinking habit, in an ignorant population, fostered coarseness, vulgarity and an indolent disregard for the social improvement of the place, so that it was admitted, by the few sober, thinking people who remained there, that St. Michael's had become a very unsaintly, as well as unsightly place, before I went there to reside.

I left Baltimore for St. Michael's in the month of March, 1833. I know the year, because it was the one succeeding the first cholera in Baltimore, and was the year, also, of that strange phenomenon, when the heavens seemed about to part with its starry train. I witnessed this gorgeous spectacle, and was awestruck. The air seemed filled with bright, descending messengers from the sky. It was about daybreak when I saw this sublime scene. I was not without the suggestion, at the moment, that it might be the harbinger of the coming of the Son of Man; and, in my then state of mind, I was prepared to hail Him as my friend and deliverer. I had read, that the "stars shall fall from heaven"; and they were now falling.

But, to my story. It was now more than seven years since I had lived with Master Thomas Auld, in the family of my old master, on Col. Lloyd's plantation. We were almost entire strangers to each other; for, when I knew him at the house of my old master, it was not as a master, but simply as "Captain Auld," who had married old master's daughter. All my lessons concerning his temper and disposition, and the best methods of pleasing him, were yet to be learnt. Slaveholders, however, are not very ceremonious in approaching a slave; and my ignorance of the new material in shape of a master was but transient. Nor was my mistress long in making known her animus. She was not a "Miss Lucretia," traces of whom I yet remembered, and the more especially, as I saw them shining in the face of little Amanda, her daughter, now living under a step-mother's government. Thomas and Rowena, I found to be a well-matched pair. He was stingy, and she was cruel; and—what was quite natural in such cases—she possessed the ability to make him as cruel as herself, while she could easily descend to the level of his meanness. In the house of Master Thomas, I was made—for the first time in seven years to feel the pinchings of hunger, and this was not very easy to bear.

For, in all the changes of Master Hugh's family, there was no change in the bountifulness with which they supplied me with food. Not to give a slave enough to eat, is meanness intensified, and it is so recognized among slaveholders generally, in Maryland. The rule is, no matter how coarse the food, only let there be enough of it.

All know the lightness of Indian cornmeal, as an article of food, and can easily judge from the following facts whether the statements I have made of the stinginess of Master Thomas, are borne out. There were four slaves of us in the kitchen, and four whites in the great house, Thomas Auld, Mrs. Auld, Hadaway Auld (brother of Thomas Auld) and little Amanda. The names of the slaves in the kitchen were Eliza, my sister; Priscilla, my aunt; Henny, my cousin; and myself. There were eight persons in the family. There was, each week, one half bushel of cornmeal brought from the mill; and in the kitchen, cornmeal was almost our exclusive food, for very little else was allowed us. Out of this bushel of cornmeal, the family in the great house had a small loaf every morning; thus leaving us, in the kitchen, with not quite a half a peck per week, apiece. This allowance was less than half the allowance of food on Lloyd's plantation. It was not enough to subsist upon; and we were, therefore, reduced to the wretched necessity of living at the expense of our neighbors. We were compelled either to beg, or to steal, and we did both.

I frankly confess, that while I hated everything like stealing, as such, I nevertheless did not hesitate to take food, when I was hungry, wherever I could find it. Nor was this practice the mere result of an unreasoning instinct; it was, in my case, the result of a clear apprehension of the claims of morality. I weighed and considered the matter closely, before I ventured to satisfy my hunger by such means. Considering that my labor and person were the property of Master Thomas, and that I was by him deprived of the necessaries of life — necessaries obtained by my own labor—it was easy to deduce the right to supply myself with what was my own. It was simply appropriating what was my own to the use of my master, since the health and strength derived from such food were exerted in his service. To be sure, this was stealing, according to the law and gospel I heard from St. Michael's pulpit; but I had already begun to attach less importance to what dropped from that quarter, on that point, while, as yet, I retained my reverence for religion.

It was not always convenient to steal from master, and the same reason why I might, innocently, steal from him, did not seem to justify me in stealing from others. In the case of my master, it was only a question of removal—the taking his meat out of one tub, and putting it into another; the ownership of the meat was not affected by the transaction. At first, he owned it in the tub, and last, he owned it in me. His meat house was not always open. There was a strict watch kept on that point, and the key was on a large bunch in Rowena's pocket. A great many times have we, poor creatures, been severely pinched with hunger, when meat and bread have been moulding under the lock, while the key was in the pocket of our mistress. This had been so when she knew we were nearly half starved; and yet, that mistress, with saintly air, would kneel with her husband, and pray each morning that a merciful God would bless them in basket and in store, and save them, at last, in his kingdom.

Bad as slaveholders are, I have seldom met with one so entirely destitute of every element of character capable of inspiring respect, as was my present master, Capt. Thomas Auld.

When I lived with him, I thought him incapable of a noble action. The leading trait in his character was intense selfishness. I think he was fully aware of this fact himself, and often tried to conceal it. Capt. Auld was not a born slaveholder—not a birthright member of the slaveholding oligarchy. He was only a slaveholder by marriage-right; and, of all slaveholders, these latter are, by far, the most exacting. There was in him all the love of domination, the pride of mastery, and the swagger of authority, but his rule lacked the vital element of consistency. He could be cruel; but his methods of showing it were cowardly, and evinced his meanness rather than his spirit. His commands were strong, his enforcement weak.

The luxury of having slaves wait upon him was something new to Master Thomas; and for it he was wholly unprepared. He was a slaveholder, without the ability to hold or manage his slaves. We seldom called him "master," but generally addressed him by his "bay craft" title—"Capt. Auld." It is easy to see that such conduct might do much to make him appear awkward, and, consequently, fretful. His wife was especially solicitous to have us call her husband "master." Is your master at the store?"—"Where is your master?"—"Go and tell your master"—"I will make your master acquainted with your conduct"—she would say; but we were inapt scholars. Especially were I and my sister Eliza inapt in this particular. Aunt Priscilla was less stubborn and defiant in her spirit than Eliza and myself; and, I think, her road was less rough than ours.

In the month of August, 1833, when I had almost become desperate under the treatment of Master Thomas, and when I entertained more strongly than ever the oft-repeated determination to run away, a circumstance occurred which seemed to promise brighter and better days for us all. At a Methodist camp-meeting, held in the Bay Side about eight miles from St. Michael's, Master Thomas came out with a profession of religion. He had long been an object of interest to the church, and to the ministers, as I had seen by the repeated visits and lengthy exhortations of the latter. He was a fish quite worth catching, for he had money and standing. In the community of St. Michael's he was equal to the best citizen. He was strictly temperate; perhaps, from principle, but most likely, from interest. There was very little to do for him, to give him the appearance of piety, and to make him a pillar in the church.

Well, the camp-meeting continued a week; people gathered from all parts of the county, and two steamboat loads came from Baltimore. The ground was happily chosen; seats were arranged; a stand erected; a rude altar fenced in, fronting the preachers' stand, with straw in it for the accommodation of mourners. This latter would hold at least one hundred persons. In front, and on the sides of the preachers' stand, and outside the long rows of seats, rose the first class of stately tents, each vying with the other in strength, neatness, and capacity for accommodating its inmates. Behind this first circle of tents was another, less imposing, which reached round the campground to the speakers' stand. Outside this second class of tents were covered wagons, ox carts, and vehicles of every shape and size. These served as tents to their owners. Outside of these, huge fires were burning, in all directions, where roasting, and boiling, and frying were going on, for the benefit of those who were attending to their own spiritual welfare within the circle. Behind the preachers' stand, a narrow space was marked out for the use of the colored people. There were no seats provided for this class of persons; the preachers addressed them, "over the left," if they addressed them at all. After the preaching was over, at every service, an invitation was given to mourners to come into the pen; and, in some cases, ministers went out to persuade men and women to come in. By one of these ministers, Master Thomas Auld was persuaded to go inside the pen. I was deeply interested in that matter, and followed; and, though colored people were not allowed either in the pen or in front of the preachers' stand, I ventured to take my stand at a sort of half-way place between the blacks and whites, where I could distinctly see the movements of mourners, and especially the progress of Master Thomas.

"If he has got religion," thought I, "he will emancipate his slaves; and if he should not do so much as this, he will, at any rate, behave toward us more kindly, and feed us more generously than he has heretofore done." Appealing to my own religious experience, and judging my master by what was true in my own case, I could not regard him as soundly converted, unless some such good results followed his profession of religion.

But in my expectations I was doubly disappointed; Master Thomas was Master Thomas still. The fruits of his righteousness were to show themselves in no such way as I had anticipated. His conversion was not to change his relation toward men—at any rate not toward BLACK men—but toward God. My faith, I confess, was not great. There was something in his appearance that, in my mind, cast a doubt over his conversion. Standing where I did, I could see his every movement. I watched narrowly while he remained in the little pen; and although I saw that his face was extremely red, and his hair disheveled, and though I heard him groan, and saw a stray tear halting on his cheek, as if inquiring "which way shall I go?"—I could not wholly confide in the genuineness of his conversion. The hesitating behavior of that teardrop and its loneliness, dis- tressed me, and cast a doubt upon the whole transaction, of which it was a part.

But people said, "Capt. Auld had come through," and it was for me to hope for the best. I was bound to do this, in charity, for I, too, was religious, and had been in the church full three years, although now I was not more than sixteen years old. Slaveholders may, sometimes, have confidence in the piety of some of their slaves; but the slaves seldom have confidence in the piety of their masters.

"He cant go to heaven with our blood in his skirts," is a settled point in the creed of every slave; rising superior to all teaching to the contrary, and standing forever as a fixed fact. The highest evidence the slaveholder can give the slave of his acceptance with God, is the emancipation of his slaves. This is proof that he is willing to give up all to God, and for the sake of God. Not to do this, was, in my estimation, and in the opinion of all the slaves, an evidence of half-heartedness, and wholly inconsistent with the idea of genuine conversion. I had read, also, somewhere in the Methodist Discipline, the following question and answer:
"Question. What shall be done for the extirpation of slavery?
"Answer. We declare that we are much as ever convinced of the great evil of slavery; therefore, no slaveholder shall be eligible to any official station in our church."

These words sounded in my ears for a long time, and encouraged me to hope. But, as I have before said, I was doomed to disappointment. Master Thomas seemed to be aware of my hopes and expectations concerning him. I have thought, before now, that he looked at me in answer to my glances, as much as to say, "I will teach you, young man, that, though I have parted with my sins, I have not parted with my sense. I shall hold my slaves, and go to heaven too."

Possibly, to convince us that we must not presume too much upon his recent conversion, he became rather more rigid and stringent in his exactions. There always was a scarcity of good nature about the man; but now his whole countenance was soured over with the seemings of piety. His religion, there- fore, neither made him emancipate his slaves, nor caused him to treat them with greater humanity. If religion had any effect on his character at all, it made him more cruel and hateful in all his ways. The natural wickedness of his heart had not been removed, but only reinforced, by the profession of religion. Do I judge him harshly? God forbid. Facts are facts. Capt. Auld made the greatest profession of piety. His house was, literally, a house of prayer. In the morning, and in the evening, loud prayers and hymns were heard there, in which both himself and his wife joined; yet, no more meal was brought from the mill, no more attention was paid to the moral welfare of the kitchen; and nothing was done to make us feel that the heart of Master Thomas was one whit better than it was before he went into the little pen, opposite to the preachers' stand, on the campground.

Our hopes soon vanished; for the authorities let him into the church at once. His house being one of the holiest, if not the happiest in St. Michael's, became the "preachers' home." These preachers evidently liked to share Master Thomas's hospitality; for while he starved us, he stuffed them. Three or four of these ambassadors of the gospel— according to slavery—have been there at a time; all living on the fat of the land, while we, in the kitchen, were nearly starving. Not often did we get a smile of recognition from these holy men. They seemed almost as unconcerned about our getting to heaven, as they were about our getting out of slavery. To this general charge there was one exception—the Rev. GEORGE COOKMAN. Unlike the other five Reverends in the St. Michael's circuit, he kindly took an interest in our temporal and spiritual welfare. Our souls and our bodies were all alike sacred in his sight; and he really had a good deal of genuine anti-slavery feeling mingled with his colonization ideas. There was not a slave in our neighborhood that did not love, and almost venerate, Mr. Cookman. It was pretty generally believed that he had been chiefly instrumental in bringing one of the largest slaveholders—Mr. Samuel Harrison—in that neighborhood, to emancipate all his slaves, and, indeed, the general impression was, that Mr. Cookman had labored faithfully with slaveholders, whenever he met them, to induce them to emancipate their bondmen, and that he did this as a religious duty.

When this good man was at our house, we were all sure to be called in to prayers in the morning; and he was not slow in making inquiries as to the state of our minds, nor in giving us a word of exhortation and of encouragement. Great was the sorrow of all the slaves, when this faithful preacher of the gospel was removed from the Talbot county circuit. He was an eloquent preacher, and possessed what few ministers, south of Mason Dixon's line, possess, or dare to show: a warm and philanthropic heart. The Mr. Cookman, of whom I speak, was an Englishman by birth, and perished while on his way to England, on board the ill-fated "President". Could the thou- sands of slaves in Maryland know the fate of the good man, to whose words of comfort they were so largely indebted, they would thank me for dropping a tear on this page, in memory of their favorite preacher, friend and benefactor.

But, let me return to Master Thomas, and to my experience, after his conversion. In Baltimore, I could, occasionally, into a Sabbath school, among the free children, and receive lessons, with the rest; but, having already learned both to read and to write, I was more of a teacher than a pupil, even there. When, however, I went back to the Eastern Shore, and was at the house of Master Thomas, I was neither allowed to teach, nor to be taught. The whole community—with but a single exception, among the whites—frowned upon everything like imparting instruction either to slaves or to free colored persons. That single exception, a pious young man named Wilson, asked me, one day, if I would like to assist him in teaching a little Sabbath school, at the house of a free colored man in St. Michael's, named James Mitchell. The idea was to me a delightful one, and I told him I would gladly devote as much of my Sabbath as I could command, to that most laudable work. Mr. Wilson soon mustered up a dozen old spelling books, and a few testaments; and we commenced operations, with some twenty scholars, in our Sunday school. Here, thought I, is something worth living for; here is an excellent chance for usefulness; and I shall soon have a company of young friends, lovers of know- ledge, like some of my Baltimore friends, from whom I now felt parted forever.

Our first Sabbath passed delightfully, and I spent the week after very joyously. I could not go to Baltimore, but I could make a little Baltimore here. At our second meeting, I learned that there was some objection to the existence of the Sabbath school; and, sure enough, we had scarcely got at work—good work, simply teaching a few colored children how to read the gospel of the Son of God—when in rushed a mob, headed by Mr. Wright Fairbanks and Mr. Garrison West—two class-leaders —

and Master Thomas; who, armed with sticks and other missiles, drove us off, and commanded us never to meet for such a purpose again. One of this pious crew told me, that as for my part, I wanted to be another Nat Turner; and if I did not look out, I should get as many balls into me, as Nat did into him. Thus ended the infant Sabbath school, in the town of St. Michael's. The reader will not be surprised when I say, that the breaking up of my Sabbath school, by these class-leaders, and professedly holy men, did not serve to strengthen my religious convictions.

The cloud over my St. Michael's home grew heavier and blacker than ever. It was not merely the agency of Master Thomas, in breaking up and destroying my Sabbath school, that shook my confidence in the power of southern religion to make men wiser or better; but I saw in him all the cruelty and meanness, after his conversion, which he had exhibited before he made a profession of religion. His cruelty and meanness were especially displayed in his treatment of my unfortunate cousin, Henny, whose lameness made her a burden to him. I have no extraordinary personal hard usage toward myself to complain of, against him, but I have seen him tie up the lame and maimed woman, and whip her in a manner most brutal, and shocking; and then, with blood-chilling blasphemy, he would quote the passage of scripture, "That servant which knew his lord's will, and prepared not himself, neither did according to his will, shall be beaten with many stripes."

Master would keep this lacerated woman tied up by her wrists, to a bolt in the joist, three, four and five hours at a time. He would tie her up early in the morning, whip her with a cowskin before breakfast; leave her tied up; go to his store, and, returning to his dinner, repeat the castigation; laying on the rugged lash, on flesh already made raw by repeated blows. He seemed desirous to get the poor girl out of existence, or, at any rate, off his hands. In proof of this, he afterwards gave her away to his sister Sarah (Mrs. Cline) but, as in the case of Master Hugh, Henny was soon returned on his hands. Finally, upon a pretense that he could do nothing with her (I use his own words) he "set her adrift, to take care of herself."

Here was a recently converted man, holding, with tight grasp, the well-framed, and able bodied slaves left him by old master—the persons, who, in freedom, could have taken care of themselves; yet, turning loose the only cripple among them, virtually to starve and die.

No doubt, had Master Thomas been asked, by some pious northern brother, why he continued to sustain the relation of a slaveholder, to those whom he retained, his answer would have been precisely the same as many other religious slaveholders have returned to that inquiry: "I hold my slaves for their own good."

Bad as my condition was when I lived with Master Thomas, I was soon to experience a life far more goading and bitter. The many differences springing up between myself and Master Thomas, owing to the clear perception I had of his character, and the boldness with which I defended myself against his capricious complaints, led him to declare that I was unsuited to his wants; that my city life had affected me perniciously; that, in fact, it had almost ruined me for every good purpose, and had fitted me for everything that was bad. One of my greatest faults, or offenses, was that of letting his horse get away, and go down to the farm belonging to his father-in-law.

The animal had a liking for that farm, with which I fully sympathized. Whenever I let it out, it would go dashing down the road to Mr. Hamilton's, as if going on a grand frolic. My horse gone, of course I must go after it. The explanation of our mutual attachment to the place is the same; the horse found there good pasturage, and I found there plenty of bread. Mr. Hamilton had his faults, but starving his slaves was not among them. He gave food, in abundance, and that, too, of an excellent quality. In Mr. Hamilton's cook—Aunt Mary—I found a most generous and considerate friend. She never allowed me to go there without giving me bread enough to make good the deficiencies of a day or two.

Master Thomas at last resolved to endure my behavior no longer; he could neither keep me, nor his horse, we liked so well to be at his father-in-law's farm. I had now lived with him nearly nine months, and he had given me a number of severe whippings, without any visible improvement in my character, or my conduct; and now he was resolved to put me out—as he said—"to be broken."

There was, in the Bay Side, very near the camp ground, where my master got his religious impressions, a man named Edward Covey, who enjoyed the execrated reputation of being a first rate hand at breaking young Negroes. This Covey was a poor man, a farm renter; and this reputation (hateful as it was to the slaves and to all good men) was, at the same time, of immense advantage to him. It enabled him to get his farm tilled with very little expense, compared with what it would have cost him without this most extraordinary reputation.

Some slaveholders thought it an advantage to let Mr. Covey have the government of their slaves a year or two, almost free of charge, for the sake of the excellent training such slaves got under his happy management! Like some horse breakers, noted for their skill, who ride the best horses in the country without expense, Mr. Covey could have under him, the most fiery bloods of the neighborhood, for the simple reward of returning them to their owners, well broken.

I was made aware of his character by some who had been under his hand; and while I could not look forward to going to him with any pleasure, I was glad to get away from St. Michael's. I was sure of getting enough to eat at Covey's, even if I suffered in other respects. This, to a hungry man, is not a prospect to be regarded with indifference.

15

Covey, the Negro Breaker

The morning of the first of January, 1834, with its chilling wind and pinching frost, quite in harmony with the winter in my own mind, found me, with my little bundle of clothing on the end of a stick swung across my shoulder, on the main road, bending my way toward Covey's, whither I had been imperiously ordered by Master Thomas. The latter had been as good as his word, and had committed me, without reserve, to the mastery of Mr. Edward Covey. Eight or ten years had now passed since I had been taken from my grandmother's cabin, in Tuckahoe; and these years, for the most part, I had spent in Baltimore, where—as the reader has already seen—I was treated with comparative tenderness. I was now about to sound profounder depths in slave life. The rigors of a field, less tolerable than the field of battle, awaited me.

My new master was notorious for his fierce and savage disposition, and my only consolation in going to live with him was, the certainty of finding him precisely as represented by common fame. There was neither joy in my heart, nor elasticity in my step, as I stated in search of the tyrant's home. Starvation made me glad to leave Thomas Auld's, and the cruel lash made me dread to go to Covey's. Escape was impossible; so, heavy and sad, I paced the seven miles, which separated Covey's house from St. Michael's—thinking much by the solitary way—averse to my condition; but thinking was all I could do. Like a fish in a net, allowed to play for a time, I was now drawn rapidly to the shore, secured at all points.

With thoughts and reflections like these, I came in sight of a small wood-colored building, about a mile from the main road, which, from the description I had received, at starting, I easily recognized as my new home. The Chesapeake bay—upon the jutting banks of which the little wood-colored house was standing—white with foam, raised by the heavy north-west wind; Poplar Island, covered with a thick, black pine forest, standing out amid this half ocean; and Kent Point, stretching its sandy, desert-like shores out into the foam-casted bay—were all in sight, and deepened the wild and desolate aspect of my new home.

The good clothes I had brought with me from Baltimore were now worn thin, and had not been replaced; for Master Thomas was as little careful to provide us against cold, as against hunger. Met here by a north wind, sweeping through an open space of forty miles, I was glad to make any port; and, there- fore, I speedily pressed on to the little wood-colored house. The family consisted of Mr. and Mrs. Covey; Miss Kemp (a broken-backed woman) a sister of Mrs. Covey; William Hughes, cousin to Edward Covey; Caroline, the cook; Bill Smith, a hired man; and myself. Bill Smith, Bill Hughes, and myself, were the working force of the farm, which consisted of three or four hundred acres. I was now, for the first time in my life, to be a field hand; and in my new employment I found myself even more awkward than a green country boy may be supposed to be, upon his first entrance into the bewildering scenes of city life; and my awkwardness gave me much trouble.

Strange and unnatural as it may seem, I had been at my new home but three days, before Mr. Covey (my brother in the Methodist church) gave me a bitter foretaste of what was in reserve for me. I presume he thought, that since he had but a single year in which to complete his work, the sooner he began, the better. Perhaps he thought that by coming to blows at once, we should mutually better understand our relations. But to whatever motive, direct or indirect, the cause may be referred, I had not been in his possession three whole days, before he subjected me to a most brutal chastisement. Under his heavy blows, blood flowed freely, and wales were left on my back as large as my little finger. The sores on my back, from this flogging, continued for weeks, for they were kept open by the rough and coarse cloth which I wore for shirting. The whole thing I found to be characteristic of the man; and I was probably treated no worse by him than scores of lads who had previously been committed to him, for reasons similar to those which induced my master to place me with him. But, here are the facts connected with the affair, precisely as they occurred.

On one of the coldest days of the whole month of January, 1834, I was ordered, at day break, to get a load of wood, from a forest about two miles from the house. In order to perform this work, Mr. Covey gave me a pair of unbroken oxen, for, it seems, his breaking abilities had not been turned in this direction; and I may remark, in passing, that working animals in the south, are seldom so well trained as in the north. In due form, and with all proper ceremony, I was introduced to this huge yoke of unbroken oxen, and was carefully told which was "Buck," and which was "Darby"—which was the "in hand," and which was the "off hand" ox. The master of this important ceremony was no less a person than Mr. Covey, himself; and the introduction was the first of the kind I had ever had. My life, hitherto, had led me away from horned cattle, and I had no knowledge of the art of managing them. What was meant by the "in ox," as against the "off ox," when both were equally fastened to one cart, and under one yoke, I could not very easily divine; and the difference, implied by the names, and the peculiar duties of each, were like Greek to me.

Why was not the "off ox" called the "in ox?" Where and what is the reason for this distinction in names, when there is none in the things themselves? After initiating me into the "woa," "back" "gee," "hither"—the entire spoken language between oxen and driver—Mr. Covey took a rope, about ten feet long and one inch thick, and placed one end of it around the horns of the "in hand ox," and gave the other end to me, telling me that if the oxen started to run away, as the scamp knew they would, I must hold on to the rope and stop them. I need not tell any one who is acquainted with either the strength of the disposition of an untamed ox, that this order was about as unreasonable as a command to shoulder a mad bull!

I had never driven oxen before, and I was as awkward as a driver, as it is possible to conceive. It did not answer for me to plead ignorance to Mr. Covey; there was something in his manner that quite forbade that. He was a man to whom a slave seldom felt any disposition to speak. Cold, distant, morose, with a face wearing all the marks of captious pride and malicious sternness, he repelled all advances. Covey was not a large man; he was only about five feet ten inches in height, I should think; short necked, round shoulders; of quick and wiry motion, of thin and wolfish visage; with a pair of small, greenish-gray eyes, set well back under a forehead without dignity, and constantly in motion, and floating his passions, rather than his thoughts, in sight, but denying them utterance in words. The creature presented an appearance altogether ferocious and sinister, disagreeable and forbidding, in the extreme. When he spoke, it was from the corner of his mouth, and in a sort of light growl, like a dog, when an attempt is made to take a bone from him.

The fellow had already made me believe him even worse than he had been presented. With his directions, and without stopping to question, I started for the woods, quite anxious to perform my first exploit in driving, in a creditable manner. The distance from the house to the woods gate a full mile, I should think—was passed over with very little difficulty; for although the animals ran, I was fleet enough, in the open field, to keep pace with them; especially as they pulled me along at the end of the rope; but, on reaching the woods, I was speedily thrown into a distressing plight. The animals took fright, and started off ferociously into the woods, carrying the cart, full tilt, against trees, over stumps, and dashing from side to side, in a manner altogether frightful. As I held the rope, I expected every moment to be crushed between the cart and the huge trees, among which they were so furiously dashing.

After running thus for several minutes, my oxen were, finally, brought to a stand, by a tree, against which they dashed themselves with great violence, upsetting the cart, and entangling themselves among sundry young saplings. By the shock, the body of the cart was flung in one direction, and the wheels and tongue in another, and all in the greatest confusion. There I was, all alone, in a thick wood, to which I was a stranger; my cart upset and shattered; my oxen entangled, wild, and enraged; and I, poor soul! but a green hand, to set all this disorder right. I knew no more of oxen than the ox driver is supposed to know of wisdom. After standing a few moments surveying the damage and disorder, and not without a presentiment that this trouble would draw after it others even more distressing, I took one end of the cart body, and, by an extra outlay of strength, I lifted it toward the axle-tree, from which it had been violently flung; and after much pulling and straining, I succeeded in getting the body of the cart in its place. This was an important step out of the difficulty, and its performance increased my courage for the work which remained to be done.

The cart was provided with an ax, a tool with which I had become pretty well acquainted in the shipyard at Baltimore. With this, I cut down the saplings by which my oxen were entangled, and again pursued my journey, with my heart in my mouth, lest the oxen should again take it into their senseless heads to cut up a caper. My fears were groundless. Their spree was over for the present, and the rascals now moved off as soberly as though their behavior had been natural and exemplary. On reaching the part of the forest where I had been, the day before, chopping wood, I filled the cart with a heavy load, as a security against another running away. But, the neck of an ox is equal in strength to iron. It defies all ordinary burdens, when excited. Tame and docile to a proverb, when well trained, the ox is the most sullen and intractable of animals when but half broken to the yoke.

I now saw, in my situation, several points of similarity with that of the oxen. They were property, so was I; they were to be broken, so was I. Covey was to break me, I was to break them; break and be broken—such is life.

Half the day already gone, and my face not yet homeward! It required only two day's experience and observation to teach me, that such apparent waste of time would not be lightly over-looked by Covey. I therefore hurried toward home; but, on reaching the lane gate, I met with the crowning disaster for the day. This gate was a fair specimen of southern handicraft. There were two huge posts, eighteen inches in diameter, rough hewed and square, and the heavy gate was so hung on one of these, that it opened only about half the proper distance. On arriving here, it was necessary for me to let go the end of the rope on the horns of the "in hand ox;" and now as soon as the gate was open, and I let go of it to get the rope, again, off went my oxen—making nothing of their load—full tilt; and in doing so they caught the huge gate between the wheel and the cart body, literally crushing it to splinters, and coming only within a few inches of subjecting me to a similar crushing, for I was just in advance of the wheel when it struck the left gate post.

With these two hair-breadth escape, I thought I could successfully explain to Mr. Covey the delay, and avert apprehended punishment.

I was not without a faint hope of being commended for the stern resolution which I had displayed in accomplishing the difficult task—a task which, I afterwards learned, even Covey himself would not have undertaken, without first driving the oxen for some time in the open field, preparatory to their going into the woods. But, in this I was disappointed. On coming to him, his countenance assumed an aspect of rigid displeasure, and, as I gave him a history of the casualties of my trip, his wolfish face, with his greenish eyes, became intensely ferocious. "Go back to the woods again," he said, muttering something else about wasting time. I hastily obeyed; but I had not gone far on my way, when I saw him coming after me. My oxen now behaved themselves with singular propriety, opposing their present conduct to my representation of their former antics. I almost wished, now that Covey was coming, they would do something in keeping with the character I had given them; but no, they had already had their spree, and they could afford now to be extra good, readily obeying my orders, and seeming to understand them quite as well as I did myself.

On reaching the woods, my torment- or—who seemed all the way to be remarking upon the good behavior of his oxen—came up to me, and ordered me to stop the cart, accompanying the same with the threat that he would now teach me how to break gates, and idle away my time, when he sent me to the woods. Suiting the action to the word, Covey paced off, in his own wiry fashion, to a large, black gum tree, the young shoots of which are generally used for ox goads, they being exceedingly tough. Three of these goads, from four to six feet long, he cut off, and trimmed up, with his large jack-knife. This done, he ordered me to take off my clothes. To this unreasonable order I made no reply, but sternly refused to take off my clothing. "If you will beat me," thought I, "you shall do so over my clothes."

After many threats, which made no impression on me, he rushed at me with something of the savage fierceness of a wolf, tore off the few and thinly worn clothes I had on, and proceeded to wear out, on my back, the heavy goads which he had cut from the gum tree. This flogging was the first of a series of floggings; and though very severe, it was less so than many which came after it, and these, for offenses far lighter than the gate breaking. I remained with Mr. Covey one year (I cannot say I lived with him) and during the first six months that I was there, I was whipped, either with sticks or cowskins, every week. Aching bones and a sore back were my constant companions.

Frequent as the lash was used, Mr. Covey thought less of it, as a means of breaking down my spirit, than that of hard and long continued labor. He worked me steadily, up to the point of my powers of endurance. From the dawn of day in the morning, till the darkness was complete in the evening, I was kept at hard work, in the field or the woods. At certain seasons of the year, we were all kept in the field till eleven and twelve o'clock at night. At these times, Covey would attend us in the field, and urge us on with words or blows, as it seemed best to him. He had, in his life, been an overseer, and he well understood the business of slave driving. There was no deceiving him. He knew just what a man or boy could do, and he held both to strict account. When he pleased, he would work himself, making everything fly before him. It was, however, scarcely necessary for Mr. Covey to be really present in the field, to have his work go on industriously. He had the faculty of making us feel that he was always present. By a series of adroitly managed surprises, which he practiced, I was pre- pared to expect him at any moment. His plan was, never to approach the spot where his hands were at work, in an open, manly and direct manner. He would creep and crawl, in ditches and gullies; hide behind stumps and bushes, and practice so much of the cunning of the serpent, that Bill Smith and I—between ourselves—never called him by any other name than "the snake." We fancied that in his eyes and his gait we could see a snakish resemblance.

One half of his proficiency in the art of Negro breaking, consisted, I should think, in this species of cunning. We were never secure. He could see or hear us nearly all the time. He was, to us, behind every stump, tree, bush and fence on the plantation. He carried this kind of trickery so far, that he would sometimes mount his horse, and make believe he was going to St. Michael's; and, in thirty minutes afterward, you might find his horse tied in the woods, and the snake-like Covey lying flat in the ditch, with his head lifted above its edge, or in a fence corner, watching every movement of the slaves! I have known him walk up to us and give us special orders, as to our work, in advance, as if he were leaving home with a view to being absent several days; and before he got half way to the house, he would avail himself of our inattention to his movements, to turn short on his heels, conceal himself behind a fence corner or a tree, and watch us until the going down of the sun.

Mean and contemptible as is all this, it is in keeping with the character which the life of a slaveholder is calculated to produce. There is no earthly inducement, in the slave's condition, to incite him to labor faithfully. The fear of punishment is the sole motive for any sort of industry with him. Knowing this fact, as the slaveholder does, and judging the slave by himself, he naturally concludes the slave will be idle whenever the cause for this fear is absent. Hence, all sorts of petty deceptions are practiced, to inspire this fear.

I have already said, or implied, that Mr. Edward Covey was a poor man. He was, in fact, just commencing to lay the foundation of his fortune, as fortune is regarded in a slave state. The first condition of wealth and respectability there, being the ownership of human property, every nerve is strained, by the poor man, to obtain it, and very little regard is had to the manner of obtaining it. In pursuit of this object, pious as Mr. Covey was, he proved himself to be as unscrupulous and base as the worst of his neighbors. In the beginning, he was only able—as he said—"to buy one slave;" and, scandalous and shocking as is the fact, he boasted that he bought her simply "as a breeder." But the worst is not told in this naked statement. This young woman (Caroline was her name) was virtually compelled by Mr. Covey to abandon herself to the object for which he had purchased her; and the result was, the birth of twins at the end of the year. At this addition to his human stock, both Edward Covey and his wife, Susan, were ecstatic with joy. No one dreamed of reproaching the woman, or of finding fault with the hired man—Bill Smith—the father of the children, for Mr. Covey himself had locked the two up together every night, thus inviting the result.

But I will pursue this revolting subject no further. No better illustration of the unchaste and demoralizing character of slavery can be found, than is furnished in the fact that this professedly Christian slaveholder, amidst all his prayers and hymns, was shamelessly and boastfully encouraging, and actually compelling, in his own house, undisguised and unmitigated fornication, as a means of increasing his human stock. I may remark here, that, while this fact will be read with disgust and shame at the north, it will be laughed at, as smart and praise-worthy in Mr. Covey at the south; for a man is no more condemned there for buying a woman and devoting her to this life of dishonor, than for buying a cow, and raising stock from her.

I will here reproduce what I said of my own experience in this wretched place, more than ten years ago:

"If at any one time of my life, more than another, I was made to drink the bitterest dregs of slavery, that time was during the first six months of my stay with Mr. Covey. We were worked all weathers. It was never too hot or too cold; it could never rain, blow, snow, or hail too hard for us to work in the field. Work, work, work, was scarcely more the order of the day than the night. The longest days were too short for him, and the shortest nights were too long for him. I was somewhat unmanageable when I first went there; but a few months of his discipline tamed me. Mr. Covey succeeded in breaking me. I was broken in body, soul and spirit. My natural elasticity was crushed; my intellect languished; the disposition to read departed; the cheerful spark that lingered about my eye died; the dark night of slavery closed in upon me; and behold a man transformed into a brute!

Sunday was my only leisure time. I spent this in a sort of beast-like stupor, between sleep and wake, under some large tree. At times, I would rise up, a flash of energetic freedom would dart through my soul, accompanied with a faint beam of hope, flickered for a moment, and then vanished. I sank down again, mourning over my wretched condition. I was sometimes prompted to take my life, and that of Covey, but was prevented by a combination of hope and fear. My sufferings on this plantation seem now like a dream rather than a stern reality.

Our house stood within a few rods of the Chesapeake bay, whose broad bosom was ever white with sails from every quarter of the habitable globe. Those beautiful vessels, robed in purest white, so delightful to the eye of freemen, were to me so many shrouded ghosts, to terrify and torment me with thoughts of my wretched condition. I have often, in the deep stillness of a summer's Sabbath, stood all alone upon the banks of that noble bay, and traced, with saddened heart and tearful eye, the countless number of sails moving off to the mighty ocean. The sight of these always affected me powerfully. My thoughts would compel utterance; and there, with no audience but the Almighty, I would pour out my soul's complaint in my rude way, with an apostrophe to the moving multitude of ships:

You are loosed from your moorings, and free;
I am fast in my chains, and am a slave!
You move merrily before the gentle gale,
and I sadly before the bloody whip!
You are freedom's swift-winged angels,
that fly around the world;
I am confined in bands of iron!

O, that I were free!
O, that I were on one of your gallant decks,
and under your protecting wing!
Alas! betwixt me and you the turbid waters roll.
Go on, go on. O that I could also go!
Could I but swim! If I could fly!
O, why was I born a man,
of whom to make a brute!

The glad ship is gone; she hides in the dim distance. I am left in the hottest hell of unending slavery.
O God, save me! God, deliver me! Let me be free! Is there any God? Why am I a slave?
I will run away. I will not stand it.
Get caught, or get clear, I'll try it.
I had as well die with ague as with fever.
I have only one life to lose.
I had as well be killed running as die standing.
Only think of it; one hundred miles straight north, and I am free!
Try it? Yes! God helping me, I will.
It cannot be that I shall live and die a slave.
I will take to the water.
This very bay shall yet bear me into freedom.
The steamboats steered in a northeast coast from North Point.
I will do the same;
and when I get to the head of the bay,
I will turn my canoe adrift,
and walk straight through Delaware into Pennsylvania.
When I get there,
I shall not be required to have a pass;
I will travel without being disturbed.
Let but the first opportunity offer,
and come what will, I am off.

Meanwhile, I will try to bear up under the yoke.
I am not the only slave in the world. Why should I fret?
I can bear as much as any of them.
Besides, I am but a boy,
and all boys are bound to some one.
It may be that my misery in slavery
will only increase my happiness when I get free.
There is a better day coming."

I shall never be able to narrate the mental experience through which I had to pass during my stay at Covey's. I was completely wrecked, changed and bewildered; goaded almost to madness at one time, and at another reconciling myself to my wretched condition. Everything in the way of kindness, which I had experienced at Baltimore; all my former hopes and aspirations for usefulness in the world, and the happy moments spent in the exercises of religion, contrasted with my then present lot, but increased my anguish.

I suffered bodily as well as mentally. I had neither sufficient time in which to eat or to sleep, except on Sundays. The overwork, and the brutal chastisements of which I was the victim, combined with that ever gnawing and soul-devouring thought—"I am a slave—a slave for life—a slave with no rational ground to hope for freedom"—rendered me a living embodiment of mental and physical wretchedness.

16

The Tyrant's Vice

You have, dear reader, seen me humbled, degraded, broken down, enslaved, and brutalized, and you understand how it was done; now let us see the converse of all this, and how it was brought about; and this will take us through the year 1834.

On one of the hottest days of the month of August, of the year just mentioned, had the reader been passing through Covey's farm, he might have seen me at work, in what is there called the "treading yard"—a yard upon which wheat is trodden out from the straw, by the horses' feet. I was there, at work, feeding the "fan," or rather bringing wheat to the fan, while Bill Smith was feeding. Our force consisted of Bill Hughes, Bill Smith, and a slave by the name of Eli; the latter having been hired for this occasion. The work was simple, and required strength and activity, rather than any skill or intelligence, and yet, to one entirely unused to such work, it came very hard. The heat was intense and overpowering, and there was much hurry to get the wheat, trodden out that day, through the fan; since, if that work was done an hour before sundown, the hands would have, according to a promise of Covey, that hour added to their night's rest. I was not behind any of them in the wish to complete the day's work before sundown, and, hence, I struggled with all my might to get the work forward. The promise of one hour's repose on a week day was sufficient to quick- en my pace, and to spur me on to extra endeavor. Besides, we had all planned to go fishing, and I certainly wished to have a hand in that. But I was disappointed, and the day turned out to be one of the bitterest I ever experienced.

About three o'clock, while the sun was pouring down his burning rays, and not a breeze was stirring, I broke down; my strength failed me; I was seized with a violent aching of the head, attended with extreme dizziness, and trembling in every limb. Finding what was coming, and feeling it would never do to stop work, I nerved myself up, and staggered on until I fell by the side of the wheat fan, feeling that the earth had fallen upon me. This brought the entire work to a dead stand. There was work for four; each one had his part to perform, and each part depended on the other, so that when one stopped, all were compelled to stop. Covey, who had now become my dread, as well as my tormentor, was at the house, about a hundred yards from where I was fanning, and instantly, upon hearing the fan stop, he came down to the treading yard, to inquire into the cause of our stopping. Bill Smith told him I was sick, and that I was unable longer to bring wheat to the fan.

I had, by this time, crawled away, under the side of a post- and-rail fence, in the shade, and was exceeding ill. The intense heat of the sun, the heavy dust rising from the fan, the stooping, to take up the wheat from the yard, together with the hurrying, to get through, had caused a rush of blood to my head. In this condition, Covey finding out where I was, came to me; and, after standing over me a while, he asked me what the matter was. I told him as well as I could, for it was with difficulty that I could speak. He then gave me a savage kick in the side, which jarred my whole frame, and commanded me to get up. The man had obtained complete control over me; and if he had commanded me to do any possible thing, I should, in my then state of mind, have endeavored to comply. I made an effort to rise, but fell back in the attempt, before gaining my feet. The brute now gave me another heavy kick, and again told me to rise. I again tried to rise, and succeeded in gaining my feet; but upon stooping to get the tub with which I was feeding the fan, I again staggered and fell to the ground; and I must have so fallen, had I been sure that a hundred bullets would have pierced me, as the consequence.

While down, in this sad condition, and perfectly helpless, the merciless Negro breaker took up the hickory slab, with which Hughes had been striking off the wheat to a level with the sides of the half bushel measure (a very hard weapon) and with the sharp edge of it, he dealt me a heavy blow on my head which made a large gash, and caused the blood to run freely, saying, at the same time, "If you have got the headache, I'll cure you." This done, he ordered me again to rise, but I made no effort to do so; for I had made up my mind that it was useless, and that the heartless monster might now do his worst; he could but kill me, and that might put me out of my misery.

Finding me unable to rise, or rather despairing of my doing so, Covey left me, with a view to getting on with the work without me. I was bleeding very freely, and my face was soon covered with my warm blood. Cruel and merciless as was the motive that dealt that blow, dear reader, the wound was fortunate for me. Bleeding was never more efficacious. The pain in my head speedily abated, and I was soon able to rise. Covey had, as I have said, now left me to my fate; and the question was, shall I return to my work, or shall I find my way to St. Michael's, and make Capt. Auld acquainted with the atrocious cruelty of his brother Covey, and beseech him to get me another master? Remembering the object he had in view, in placing me under the management of Covey, and further, his cruel treatment of my poor crippled cousin, Henny, and his meanness in the matter of feeding and clothing his slaves, there was little ground to hope for a favorable reception at the hands of Capt. Thomas Auld. Nevertheless, I resolved to go straight to Capt. Auld, thinking that, if not animated by motives of humanity, he might be induced to interfere on my behalf from selfish considerations. "He cannot," thought I, "allow his property to be thus bruised and battered, marred and defaced; and I will go to him, and tell him the simple truth about the matter."

In order to get to St. Michael's, by the most favorable and direct road, I must walk seven miles; and this, in my sad condition, was no easy performance. I had already lost much blood; I was exhausted by over exertion; my sides were sore from the heavy blows planted there by the stout boots of Mr. Covey; and I was, in every way, in an unfavorable plight for the journey. I however watched my chance, while the cruel and cunning Covey was looking in an opposite direction, and started off, across the field, for St. Michael's. This was a daring step; if it failed, it would only exasperate Covey, and increase the rigors of my bondage, during the remainder of my term of service under him; but the step was taken, and I must go for- ward. I succeeded in getting nearly half way across the broad field, toward the woods, before Mr. Covey observed me. I was still bleeding, and the exertion of running had started the blood afresh. "Come back! Come back!" vociferated Covey, with threats of what he would do if I did not return instantly. But, disregarding his calls and his threats, I pressed on toward the woods as fast as my feeble state would allow.

Seeing no signs of my stopping, Covey caused his horse to be brought out and saddled, as if he intended to pursue me. The race was now to be an unequal one; and, thinking I might be overhauled by him, if I kept the main road, I walked nearly the whole distance in the woods, keeping far enough from the road to avoid detection and pursuit. But, I had not gone far, before my little strength again failed me, and I laid down. The blood was still oozing from the wound in my head; and, for a time, I suffered more than I can describe. There I was, in the deep woods, sick and emaciated, pursued by a wretch whose character for revolting cruelty beggars all opprobrious speech—bleeding, and almost bloodless. I was not without the fear of bleeding to death. The thought of dying in the woods, all alone, and of being torn to pieces by the buzzards, had not yet been rendered tolerable by my many troubles and hardships, and I was glad when the shade of the trees, and the cool evening breeze, combined with my matted hair to stop the flow of blood.

After lying there about three quarters of an hour, brooding over the singular and mournful lot to which I was doomed, I again took up my journey toward St. Michael's, more weary and sad than in the morning when I left Thomas Auld's for the home of Mr. Covey. I was barefooted and bareheaded, and in my shirt sleeves. The way was through bogs and briers, and I tore my feet often during the journey. I was full five hours in going the seven or eight miles; partly, because of the difficulties of the way, and partly, because of the feebleness induced by my illness, bruises and loss of blood. On gaining my master's store, I presented an appearance of wretchedness and woe, fitted to move any but a heart of stone. From the crown of my head to the sole of my feet, there were marks of blood. My hair was all clotted with dust and blood, and the back of my shirt was literally stiff with the same. Briers and thorns had scarred and torn my feet and legs, leaving blood marks there. Had I escaped from a den of tigers, I could not have looked worse than I did on reaching St. Michael's. In this unhappy plight, I appeared before my professedly Christian master, humbly to invoke the interposition of his power and authority, to protect me from further abuse and violence. I told him all the circumstances, as well as I could; how I was endeavoring to please Covey; how hard I was at work in the present instance; how unwilling I sunk down under the heat, toil and pain; the brutal manner in which Covey had kicked me in the side; the gash cut in my head; my hesitation about troubling him (Capt. Auld) with complaints; but, that now I felt it would not be best longer to conceal from him the outrages committed on me from time to time by Covey. At first, master Thomas seemed somewhat affected by the story of my wrongs, but he soon repressed his feelings and became cold as iron. It was impossible—as I stood before him at the first —for him to seem indifferent. I distinctly saw his human nature asserting its conviction against the slave system, which made cases like mine possible; but, as I have said, humanity fell before the systematic tyranny of slavery. He first walked the floor, apparently much agitated by my story, and the sad spectacle I presented; but, presently, it was his turn to talk. He began moderately, by finding excuses for Covey, and ending with a full justification of him, and a passionate condemnation of me.

"He had no doubt I deserved the flogging. He did not believe I was sick; I was only endeavoring to get rid of work. My dizziness was laziness, and Covey did right to flog me, as he had done." After thus fairly annihilating me, and rousing himself by his own eloquence, he fiercely demanded what I wished him to do in the case!

With such a complete knock-down to all my hopes, as he had given me, and feeling, as I did, my entire subjection to his power, I had very little heart to reply. I must not affirm my innocence of the allegations which he had piled up against me; for that would be impudence, and would probably call down fresh violence as well as wrath upon me. The guilt of a slave is always, and everywhere, presumed; and the innocence of the slaveholder or the slave employer, is always asserted. The word of the slave, against this presumption, is generally treated as impudence, worthy of punishment. "Do you contradict me, you rascal?" is a final silencer of counter statements from the lips of a slave.

Calming down a little in view of my silence and hesitation, and, perhaps, from a rapid glance at the picture of misery I presented, he inquired again, "what I would have him do?" Thus invited a second time, I told Master Thomas I wished him to allow me to get a new home and to find a new master; that, as sure as I went back to live with Mr. Covey again, I should be killed by him; that he would never forgive my coming to him (Capt. Auld) with a complaint against him (Covey); that, since I had lived with him, he almost crushed my spirit, and I believed that he would ruin me for future service; that my life was not safe in his hands. This, Master Thomas regarded as "nonsense." "There was no danger of Mr. Covey's killing me; he was a good man, industrious and religious, and he would not think of removing me from that home; besides," said he and this I found was the most distressing thought of all to him—"if you should leave Covey now, that your year has but half expired, I should lose your wages for the entire year. You belong to Mr. Covey for one year, and you must go back to him, come what will. You must not trouble me with any more stories about Mr. Covey; and if you do not go immediately home, I will get hold of you myself."

This was just what I expected, when I found he had prejudged the case against me. "But, Sir," I said, "I am sick and tired, and I cannot get home tonight." At this, he again relented, and finally he allowed me to remain all night at St. Michael's; but said I must be off early in the morning, and concluded his directions by making me swallow a huge dose of epsom salts—about the only medicine ever administered to slaves.

It was quite natural for Master Thomas to presume I was feigning sickness to escape work, for he probably thought that were he in the place of a slave with no wages for his work, no praise for well doing, no motive for toil but the lash—he would try every possible scheme by which to escape labor. I say I have no doubt of this; the reason is, that there are not, under the whole heavens, a set of men who cultivate such an intense dread of labor as do the slaveholders. The charge of laziness against the slave is ever on their lips, and is the standing apology for every species of cruelty and brutality. These men literally "bind heavy burdens, grievous to be borne, and lay them on men's shoulders; but they, themselves, will not move them with one of their fingers."

17

The Last Flogging

Sleep itself does not always come to the relief of the weary in body, and the broken in spirit; especially when past troubles only foreshadow coming disasters. The last hope had been extinguished. My master, who I did not venture to hope would protect me as a man, had even now refused to protect me as his property; and had cast me back.

I remained all night—sleep I did not—at St. Michael's; and in the morning (Saturday) I started off, according to the order of Master Thomas, feeling that I had no friend on earth, and doubting if I had one in heaven. I reached

Covey's about nine o'clock; and just as I stepped into the field, before I had reached the house, Covey, true to his snakish habits, darted out at me from a fence corner, in which he had secreted himself, for the purpose of securing me. He was amply provided with a cowskin and a rope; and he evidently intended to tie me up, and to wreak his vengeance on me to the fullest extent. I should have been an easy prey, had he succeeded in getting his hands upon me, for I had taken no refreshment since noon on Friday; and this, together with the pelting, excitement, and the loss of blood, had reduced my strength. I, however, darted back into the woods, before the ferocious hound could get hold of me, and buried myself in a thicket, where he lost sight of me. The cornfield afforded me cover, in getting to the woods. But for the tall corn, Covey would have overtaken me, and made me his captive. He seemed very much chagrined that he did not catch me, and gave up the chase, very reluctantly; for I could see his angry movements, toward the house from which he had sallied, on his foray.

Well, now I am clear of Covey, and of his wrathful lash, for present. I am in the wood, buried in its somber gloom, and hushed in its solemn silence; hid from all human eyes; shut in with nature and nature's God, and absent from all human contrivances. Here was a good place to pray; to pray for help for deliverance—a prayer I had often made before. But how could I pray? Covey could pray—Capt. Auld could pray—I would fain pray; but doubts prevented my embracing the opportunity, as a religious one. Life, in itself, had almost become burdensome to me. All my outward relations were against me; I must stay here and starve (I was already hungry) or go home to Covey's, and have my flesh torn to pieces, and my spirit humbled under the cruel lash of Covey. This was the painful alternative presented to me.

The day was long and irksome. My physical condition was deplorable. I was weak from the toils of the previous day, and from the want of food and rest; and had been so little concerned about my appearance, that I had not yet washed the blood from my garments. I was an object of horror, even to myself. Life in Baltimore, when most oppressive, was a paradise to this. What had I done, what had my parents done, that such a life as this should be mine? That day, in the woods, I would have exchanged my manhood for the brutehood of an ox.

Night came. I was still in the woods, unresolved what to do. Hunger had not yet pinched me to the point of going home, and I laid myself down in the leaves to rest; for I had been watching for hunters all day, but not being molested during the day, I expected no disturbance during the night. I had come to the conclusion that Covey relied upon hunger to drive me home; and in this I was quite correct—the facts showed that he had made no effort to catch me, since morning.

During the night, I heard the step of a man in the woods. He was coming toward the place where I lay. A person lying still has the advantage over one walking in the woods, in the day time, and this advantage is much greater at night. I was not able to engage in a physical struggle, and I had recourse to the common resort of the weak. I hid myself in the leaves to prevent discovery. But, as the night rambler in the woods drew nearer, I found him to be a friend, not an enemy; it was a slave of Mr. William Groomes, of Easton, a kind hearted fellow, named "Sandy." Sandy lived with Mr. Kemp that year, about four miles from St. Michael's. He, like myself had been hired out by the year; but, unlike myself, had not been hired out to be broken. Sandy was the husband of a free woman, who lived in the lower part of "Potpie Neck," and he was now on his way through the woods, to see her, and to spend the Sabbath with her.

As soon as I had ascertained that the disturber of my solitude was not an enemy, I came out from my hiding place, and made myself known to him. I explained the circumstances of the past two days, which had driven me to the woods, and he deeply compassionated my distress. It was a bold thing for him to shelter me, and I could not ask him to do so; for, had I been found in his hut, he would have suffered the penalty of thirty- nine lashes on his bare back, if not something worse. But Sandy was too generous to permit the fear of punishment to prevent his relieving a brother bondman from hunger and exposure; and, therefore, on his own motion, I accompanied him to his home, or rather to the home of his wife—for the house and lot were hers. His wife was called up—for it was now about midnight—a fire was made, some Indian meal was soon mixed with salt and water, and an ash cake was baked in a hurry to relieve my hunger.

Sandy's wife was not behind him in kindness—both seemed to esteem it a privilege to succor me; for, although I was hated by Covey and by my master, I was loved by the colored people, because they thought I was hated for my knowledge, and persecuted because I was feared. I was the only slave now in that region who could read and write. There had been one other man, belonging to Mr. Hugh Hamilton, who could read (his name was "Jim"), but he, poor fellow, had, shortly after my coming into the neighborhood, been sold off to the far south. I saw Jim ironed, in the cart, to be carried to Easton for sale—pinioned like a yearling for the slaughter. My knowledge was now the pride of my brother slaves; and, no doubt, Sandy felt something of the general interest in me on that account.

The supper was soon ready, and though I have feasted since, with honorables, lord mayors and aldermen, over the sea, my supper on ash cake and cold water, with Sandy, was the meal, of all my life, most sweet to my taste, and now most vivid in my memory.

Supper over, Sandy and I went into a discussion of what was possible for me, under the perils and hardships which now overshadowed my path. The question was, must I go back to Covey, or must I now tempt to run away? Upon a careful survey, the latter was found to be impossible; for I was on a narrow neck of land, every avenue from which would bring me in sight of pursuers. There was the Chesapeake bay to the right, and "Pot-pie" river to the left, and St. Michael's and its neighborhood occupying the only space through which there was any retreat.

I found Sandy an old advisor. He was not only a religious man, but he professed to believe in a system for which I have no name. He was a genuine African, and had inherited some of the so-called magical powers, said to be possessed by African and eastern nations. He told me that he could help me; that, in those very woods, there was an herb, which in the morning might be found, possessing all the powers required for my protection (I put his thoughts in my own language); and that, if I would take his advice, he would procure me the root of the herb of which he spoke. He told me further, that if I would take that root and wear it on my right side, it would be impossible for Covey to strike me a blow; that with this root about my person, no white man could whip me. He said he had carried it for years, and that he had fully tested its virtues. He had never received a blow from a slaveholder since he carried it; and he never expected to receive one, for he always meant to carry that root as a protection. He knew Covey well and he had heard of the barbarous treatment to which I was subjected, and he wanted to do something for me.

Now all this talk about the root was to me very absurd and ridiculous, if not positively sinful. I at first rejected the idea that the simple carrying a root on my right side could possess any such magic power as he ascribed to it, and I was, therefore, not disposed to cumber my pocket with it. I had a positive aversion to all pretenders to "divination." It was beneath one of my intelligence to countenance such dealings with the devil, as this power implied. But, with all my learning, Sandy was more than a match for me. "My book learning," he said, "had not kept Covey off me" (a powerful argument just then) and he entreated me, with flashing eyes, to try this. If it did me no good, it could do me no harm, and it would cost me nothing, anyway.

Sandy was so earnest, and so confident of the good qualities of this weed, that, to please him, rather than from any conviction of its excellence, I was induced to take it. He had been to me the good Samaritan, and had, almost providentially, found me, and helped me when I could not help myself; how did I know but that the hand of the Lord was in it? With thoughts of this sort, I took the roots from Sandy, and put them in my right hand pocket.

This was, of course, Sunday morning. Sandy now urged me to go home, with all speed, and to walk up bravely to the house, as though nothing had happened. I saw in Sandy too deep an insight into human nature, with all his superstition, not to have some respect for his advice; and perhaps, too, a slight gleam or shadow of his superstition had fallen upon me. At any rate, I started off toward Covey's, as directed by Sandy.

Having, the previous night, poured my griefs into Sandy's ears, and got him enlisted in my behalf, having made his wife a sharer in my sorrows, and having, also, become well refreshed by sleep and food, I moved off, quite courageously, toward the much dreaded Covey's. Singularly enough, just as I entered his yard gate, I met him and his wife, dressed in their Sunday best—looking as smiling as angels—on their way to church. The manner of Covey astonished me. There was something really benignant in his countenance. He spoke to me as never before; told me that the pigs had got into the lot, and he wished me to drive them out; inquired how I was, and seemed an altered man.

This extraordinary conduct of Covey, really made me begin to think that Sandy's herb had more virtue in it than I, in my pride, had been willing to allow; and, had the day been other than Sunday, I should have attributed Covey's altered manner solely to the magic power of the root. I suspected, however, that the Sabbath, and not the root, was the real explanation of Covey's manner. His religion hindered him from breaking the Sabbath, but not from breaking my skin. He had more respect for the day than for the man, for whom the day was mercifully given; for while he would cut and slash my body during the week, he would not hesitate, on Sunday, to teach me the value of my soul, or the way of life and salvation by Jesus Christ.

All went well with me till Monday morning; and then, whether the root had lost its virtue, or whether my tormentor had gone deeper into the black art than myself (as was sometimes said of him), or whether he had obtained a special indulgence, for his faithful Sabbath day's worship, it is not necessary for me to know, or to inform the reader; but, this I may say—the pious and benignant smile which graced Covey's face on Sunday, wholly disappeared on Monday.

Long before daylight, I was called up to go and feed, rub, and curry the horses. I obeyed the call, and would have so obeyed it, had it been made at an earlier hour, for I had brought my mind to a firm resolve, during that Sunday's reflection: to obey every order, however unreasonable, if it were possible, and, if Mr. Covey should then undertake to beat me, to defend and protect myself to the best of my ability. My religious views on the subject of resisting my master, had suffered a serious shock, by
the savage persecution to which I had been subjected, and my hands were no longer tied by my religion. Master Thomas's indifference had served the last link. I had now to this extent "backslidden" from this point in the slave's religious creed; and I soon had occasion to make my fallen state known to my Sunday-pious brother, Covey.
Whilst I was obeying his order to feed and get the horses ready for the field, and when in the act of going up the stable loft for the purpose of throwing down some blades, Covey sneaked into the stable, in his peculiar snake-like way, and seizing me suddenly by the leg, he brought me to the stable floor, giving my newly mended body a fearful jar. I now forgot my roots, and

remembered my pledge to stand up in my own defense. The brute was endeavoring skillfully to get a slip-knot on my legs, before I could draw up my feet. As soon as I found what he was up to, I gave a sudden spring (my two day's rest had been of much service to me,) and by that means, no doubt, he was able to bring me to the floor so heavily. He was defeated in his plan of tying me.

While down, he seemed to think he had me very securely in his power. He little thought he was—as the rowdies say—"in" for a "rough and tumble" fight; but such was the fact. Whence came the daring spirit necessary to grapple with a man who, eight-and-forty hours before, could, with his slightest word have made me tremble like a leaf in a storm, I do not know; at any rate, I was resolved to fight, and, what was better still, I was actually hard at it. The fighting madness had come upon me, and I found my strong fingers firmly attached to the throat of my cowardly tormentor; as heedless of consequences, at the moment, as though we stood as equals before the law. The very color of the man was forgotten. I felt as supple as a cat, and was ready for the snakish creature at every turn. Every blow of his was parried, though I dealt no blows in turn. I was strictly on the defensive, preventing him from injuring me, rather than trying to injure him. I flung him on the ground several times, when he meant to have hurled me there. I held him so firmly by the throat, that his blood followed my nails. He held me, and I held him.

All was fair, thus far, and the contest was about equal. My resistance was entirely unexpected, and Covey was taken all aback by it, for he trembled in every limb. "Are you going to resist, you scoundrel?" said he. To which, I returned a polite "Yes sir;" steadily gazing my interrogator in the eye, to meet the first approach or dawning of the blow, which I expected my answer would call forth.

But, the conflict did not long remain thus equal. Covey soon cried out lustily for help; not that I was obtaining any marked advantage over him, or was injuring him, but because he was gaining none over me, and was not able, single handed, to conquer me. He called for his cousin Hughs, to come to his assistance, and now the scene was changed. I was compelled to give blows, as well as to parry them; and, since I was, in any case, to suffer for resistance, I felt (as the musty proverb goes) that "I might as well be hanged for an old sheep as a lamb." I was still defensive toward Covey, but aggressive toward Hughs; and, at the first approach of the latter, I dealt a blow, in my desperation, which fairly sickened my youthful assailant. He went off, bending over with pain, and manifesting no disposition to come within my reach again. The poor fellow was in the act of trying to catch and tie my right hand, and while flattering himself with success, I gave him the kick which sent him staggering away in pain, at the same time that I held Covey with a firm hand.

Taken completely by surprise, Covey seemed to have lost his usual strength and coolness. He was frightened, and stood puffing and blowing, seemingly unable to command words or blows. When he saw that poor Hughes was standing half bent with pain—his courage quite gone the cowardly tyrant asked if I "meant to persist in my resistance." I told him "I did mean to resist, come what might;" that I had been by him treated like a brute, during the last six months; and that I should stand it no longer. With that, he gave me a shake, and attempted to drag me toward a stick of wood, that was lying just outside the stable door. He meant to knock me down with it; but, just as he leaned over to get the stick, I seized him with both hands by the collar, and, with a vigorous and sudden snatch, I brought my assailant harmlessly, his full length, on the not over clean ground —for we were now in the cow yard. He had selected the place for the fight, and it was but right that he should have all the advantages of his own selection.

By this time, Bill, the hired man, came home. He had been to Mr. Hemsley's, to spend the Sunday with his nominal wife, and was coming home on Monday morning, to go to work. Covey and I had been skirmishing from before daybreak, till now, that the sun was almost shooting his beams over the eastern woods, and we were still at it. I could not see where the matter was to terminate. He evidently was afraid to let me go, lest I should again make off to the woods; otherwise, he would probably have obtained arms from the house, to frighten me. Holding me, Covey called upon Bill for assistance. The scene here had something comic about it. "Bill," who knew precisely what Covey wished him to do, affected ignorance, and pretended he did not know what to do.

"What shall I do, Mr. Covey," said Bill.
"Take hold of him—take hold of him!" said Covey.

With a toss of his head, peculiar to Bill, he said, "indeed, Mr. Covey I want to go to work."
"This is your work," said Covey; "take hold of him." Bill replied, with spirit, "My master hired me here to work, and not to help you whip Frederick."

It was now my turn to speak.

"Bill," said I, "don't put your hands on me."
To which he replied, "My GOD! Frederick, I ain't goin' to tech ye," and Bill walked off, leaving Covey and myself to settle our matters as best we might.

But, my present advantage was threatened when I saw Caroline (the slave-woman of Covey) coming to the cow yard to milk, for she was a powerful woman, and could have mastered me very easily, exhausted as I now was. As soon as she came into the yard, Covey attempted to rally her to his aid. Strangely—and, I may add, fortunately—Caroline was in no humor to take a hand in any such sport. We were all in open rebellion that morning.

Caroline answered the command of her master to "take hold of me," precisely as Bill had answered, but in her, it was at greater peril so to answer; she was the slave of Covey, and he could do what he pleased with her. It was not so with Bill, and Bill knew it. Samuel Harris, to whom Bill belonged, did not allow his slaves to be beaten, unless they were guilty of some crime which the law would punish. But, poor Caroline, like myself, was at the mercy of the merciless Covey; nor did she escape the dire effects of her refusal. He gave her several sharp blows.

Covey at length (two hours had elapsed) gave up the contest. Letting me go, he said—puffing and blowing at a great rate—"Now, you scoundrel, go to your work; I would not have whipped you half so much as I have had you not resisted."

The fact was, he had not whipped me at all. He had not, in all the scuffle, drawn a single drop of blood from me. I had drawn blood from him; and, even without this satisfaction, I should have been victorious, because my aim had not been to injure him, but to prevent his injuring me.

During the whole six months that I lived with Covey, after this transaction, he never laid on me the weight of his finger in anger. He would, occasionally, say he did not want to have to get hold of me again—a declaration which I had no difficulty in believing; and I had a secret feeling, which answered, "You need not wish to get hold of me again, for you will be likely to come off worse in a second fight than you did in the first."

Well, my dear reader, this battle with Mr. Covey— undignified as it was, and as I fear my narration of it is— was the turning point in my "life as a slave." It rekindled in my breast the smoldering embers of liberty; it brought up my Baltimore dreams, and revived a sense of my own manhood. I was a changed being after that fight. I was nothing before; I WAS A MAN NOW. It recalled to life my crushed self-respect and my self-confidence, and inspired me with a renewed determination to be A FREEMAN.

This spirit made me a freeman in fact, while I remained a slave in form. When a slave cannot be flogged, he is more than half free. He has a domain as broad as his own manly heart to defend, and he is really "a power on earth."

From this time, until that of my escape from slavery, I was never fairly whipped. Several attempts were made to whip me, but they were always unsuccessful. Bruises I did get, as I shall hereafter inform the reader; but the case I have been de- scribing, was the end of the brutification to which slavery had subjected me.

The reader will be glad to know why, after I had so grievously offended Mr. Covey, he did not have me taken in hand by the authorities; indeed, why the law of Maryland, which assigns hanging to the slave who resists his master, was not put in force against me; at any rate, why I was not taken up, as is usual in such cases, and publicly whipped, for an example to other slaves, and as a means of deterring me from committing the same offense again. I confess, that the easy manner in which I got off, for a long time, a surprise to me, and I cannot, even now, fully explain the cause. The only explanation I can venture to suggest, is the fact, that Covey was, probably, ashamed to have it known and confessed that he had been mastered by a boy of sixteen. Mr. Covey enjoyed the unbounded and very valuable reputation, of being a first rate overseer and Negro breaker. By means of this reputation, he was able to procure his hands for very trifling compensation, and with very great ease. His interest and his pride mutually suggested the wisdom of passing the matter by, in silence. The story that he had undertaken to whip a lad, and had been resisted, was, of itself, sufficient to damage him; for his bearing should, in the estimation of slaveholders, be of that imperial order that should make such an occurrence impossible. I judge from these circumstances, that Covey deemed it best to give me the go-by.

18

New Relations and Duties

My term of actual service to Mr. Edward Covey ended on Christmas day, 1834. I gladly left the snakish Covey, although he was now as gentle as a lamb. My home for the year 1835 was already secured—my next master was already selected. There is always more or less excitement about the matter of changing hands, but I had become somewhat reckless. I cared very little into whose hands I fell—I meant to fight my way. Despite of Covey, too, the report got abroad, that I was hard to whip; that I was guilty of kicking back; that though generally a good tempered Negro, I sometimes "got the devil in me." These sayings were rife in Talbot county, and they distinguished me among my servile brethren. Slaves, generally, will fight each other, and die at each other's hands; but there are few who are not held in awe by a white man.

Trained from the cradle up, to think and feel that their masters are superior, and invested with a sort of sacredness, there are few who can outgrow or rise above the control which that sentiment exercises. I had now got free from it, and the thing was known. One bad sheep will spoil a whole flock. Among the slaves, I was a bad sheep. I hated slavery, slaveholders, and all pertaining to them; and I did not fail to inspire others with the same feeling, wherever and whenever opportunity was presented. This made me a marked lad among the slaves, and a suspected one among the slaveholders. A knowledge of my ability to read and write, got pretty widely spread, which was very much against me.

The days between Christmas day and New Year's, are allowed the slaves as holidays. During these days, all regular work was suspended, and there was nothing to do but to keep fires, and look after the stock. This time was regarded as our own, by the grace of our masters, and we, therefore used it, or abused it, as we pleased. Those who had families at a distance, were now expected to visit them, and to spend with them the entire week. The younger slaves, or the unmarried ones, were expected to see to the cattle, and attend to incidental duties at home. The holidays were variously spent. The sober, thinking and industrious ones of our number, would employ themselves in manufacturing corn brooms, mats, horse collars and baskets, and some of these were very well made. Another class spent their time in hunting opossums, coons, rabbits, and other game. But the majority spent the holidays in sports, ball playing, wrestling, boxing, running foot races, dancing, and drinking whisky; and this latter mode of spending the time was generally most agreeable to their masters.

A slave who would work during the holidays, was thought, by his master, undeserving of holidays. Such an one had rejected the favor of his master. There was, in this simple act of continued work, an accusation against slaves; and a slave could not help thinking, that if he made three dollars during the holidays, he might make three hundred during the year. Not to be drunk during the holidays, was disgraceful; and he was esteemed a lazy and improvident man, who could not afford to drink whisky during Christmas.

The fiddling, dancing and "jubilee beating," was going on in all directions. This latter performance is strictly southern. It supplies the place of a violin, or of other musical instruments, and is played so easily, that almost every farm has its "Juba" beater. The performer improvises as he beats, and sings his merry songs, so ordering the words as to have them fall pat with the movement of his hands.

Judging from my own observation and experience, I believe these holidays to be among the most effective means, in the hands of slaveholders, of keeping down the spirit of insurrection among the slaves.

To enslave men, successfully and safely, it is necessary to have their minds occupied with thoughts and aspirations short of the liberty of which they are deprived. A certain degree of attainable good must be kept before them. These holidays serve the purpose of keeping the minds of the slaves occupied with prospective pleasure, within the limits of slavery. The young man can go wooing; the married man can visit his wife; the father and mother can see their children; the industrious and money loving can make a few dollars; the great wrestler can win laurels; the young people can meet, and enjoy each other's society; the drunken man can get plenty of whisky; and the religious man can hold prayer meetings, preach, pray and exhort during the holidays. Before the holidays, these are pleasures in prospect; after the holidays, they become pleasures of memory, and they serve to keep out thoughts and wishes of a more dangerous character.

These holidays are conductors or safety valves to carry off the explosive elements inseparable from the human mind, when reduced to the condition of slavery. But for these holidays, the rigors of bondage would become too severe for endurance, and the slave would be forced up to dangerous desperation. Woe to the slaveholder when he undertakes to hinder or to prevent the operation of these electric conductors. A succession of earthquakes would be less destructive, than the insurrectionary fires which would be sure to burst forth in different parts of the south, from such interference.

Thus, the holidays, became part and parcel of the gross fraud, wrongs and inhumanity of slavery. Ostensibly, they are institutions of benevolence, designed to mitigate the rigors of slave life, but, practically, they are a fraud. The slave's happiness is not the end sought, but, rather, the master's safety. It is not from a generous unconcern for the slave's labor that this cessation from labor is allowed, but from a prudent regard to the safety of the slave system. I am strengthened in this opinion, by the fact, that most slaveholders like to have their slaves spend the holidays in such a manner as to be of no real benefit to the slaves. It is plain, that everything like rational enjoyment among the slaves, is frowned upon; and only those wild and low sports, peculiar to semi-civilized people, are encouraged. All the license allowed, appears to have no other object than to disgust the slaves with their temporary freedom, and to make them as glad to return to their work, as they were to leave it. By plunging them into exhausting depths of drunkenness and dissipation, this effect is almost certain to follow.

I have known slaveholders resort to cunning tricks, with a view of getting their slaves deplorably drunk. A usual plan is, to make bets on a slave, that he can drink more whisky than any other; and so to induce a rivalry among them. The scenes, brought about in this way, were often scandalous and loathsome in the extreme. Whole multitudes might be found stretched out in brutal drunkenness, at once helpless and dis- gusting. Thus, when the slave asks for a few hours of virtuous freedom, his cunning master takes advantage of his ignorance, and cheers him with a dose of vicious and revolting dissipation, artfully labeled with the name of LIBERTY.

We were induced to drink, I among the rest, and when the holidays were over, we all staggered up from our filth and wallowing, took a long breath, and went away to our various fields of work; feeling, upon the whole, rather glad to go from that which our masters artfully deceived us into the belief was freedom, back again to the arms of slavery. It was about as well to be a slave to master, as to be a slave to rum and whisky.

I am the more induced to take this view of the holiday system, adopted by slaveholders, from what I know of their treatment of slaves, in regard to other things. It is the commonest thing for them to try to disgust their slaves with what they do not want them to have, or to enjoy. A slave, for instance, likes molasses; he steals some; to cure him of the taste for it, his master, in many cases, will go away to town, and buy a large quantity of the poorest quality, and set it before his slave, and, with whip in hand, compel him to eat it, until the poor fellow is made to sicken at the very thought of molasses.

The same course is often adopted to cure slaves of the disagreeable and inconvenient practice of asking for more food, when their allowance has failed them. The same disgusting process works well, too, in other things, but I need not cite them. When a slave is drunk, the slaveholder has no fear that he will plan an insurrection; no fear that he will escape to the north. It is the sober, thinking slave who is dangerous, and needs the vigilance of his master, to keep him a slave. But, to proceed with my narrative.

On the first of January, 1835, I proceeded from St. Michael's to Mr. William Freeland's, my new home. Mr. Freeland lived only three miles from St. Michael's, on an old worn out farm, which required much labor to restore it to anything like a self- supporting establishment.

I was not long in finding Mr. Freeland to be a very different man from Mr. Covey. Though not rich, Mr. Freeland was what may be called a well-bred southern gentleman, as different from Covey, as a well-trained and hardened Negro breaker is from the best specimen of the first families of the south. Though Freeland was a slaveholder, and shared many of the vices of his class, he seemed alive to the sentiment of honor. He had some sense of justice, and some feelings of humanity. He was fretful, impulsive and passionate, but I must do him the justice to say, he was free from the mean and selfish characteristics which distinguished the creature from which I had now, happily, escaped. He was open, frank, imperative, and practiced no concealments, disdaining to play the spy. In all this, he was the opposite of the crafty Covey.

Among the many advantages gained in my change from Covey's to Freeland's—startling as the statement may be—was the fact that the latter gentleman made no profession of religion. I assert most unhesitatingly, that the religion of the south—as I have observed it and proved it—is a mere covering for the most horrid crimes; the justifier of the most appalling barbarity; a sanctifier of the most hateful frauds; and a secure shelter, under which the darkest, foulest, grossest, and most infernal abominations fester and flourish. Were I again to be reduced to the condition of a slave, next to that calamity, I should regard the fact of being the slave of a religious slaveholder, the greatest that could befall me. For all slaveholders with whom I have ever met, religious slaveholders are the worst. I have found them, almost invariably, the vilest, meanest and basest of their class. Exceptions there may be, but this is true of religious slaveholders, as a class. It is not for me to explain the fact. Others may do that; I simply state it as a fact, and leave the theological, and psychological inquiry, which it raises, to be decided by others more competent than myself.

Religious slaveholders, like religious persecutors, are ever extreme in their malice and violence. I beg to introduce the reader to REV. RIGBY HOPKINS. Mr.

Hopkins resides between Easton and St. Michael's, in Talbot county, Maryland. The severity of this man made him a perfect terror to the slaves of his neighborhood. The peculiar feature of his government was, his system of whipping slaves in advance of deserving it. He always managed to have one or two slaves to whip on Monday morning, so as to start his hands to their work, under the inspiration of a new assurance on Monday, that his preaching about kindness, mercy, brotherly love, and the like, on Sunday, did not interfere with, or prevent him from establishing his authority, by the cowskin.

He seemed to wish to assure them, that his tears over poor, lost and ruined sinners, and his pity for them, did not reach to the blacks who tilled his fields. This saintly Hopkins used to boast, that he was the best hand to manage a Negro in the county. He whipped for the smallest offenses, by way of preventing the commission of large ones.

The reader might imagine a difficulty in finding faults enough for such frequent whipping. But this is because you have no idea how easy a matter it is to offend a man who is on the look-out for offenses. The man, unaccustomed to slaveholding, would be astonished to observe how many foggable offenses there are in the slaveholder's catalogue of crimes; and how easy it is to commit any one of them, even when the slave least intends it. A slaveholder, bent on finding fault, will hatch up a dozen a day, if he chooses to do so, and each one of these shall be of a punishable description. A mere look, word, or motion, a mistake, accident, or want of power, are all matters for which a slave may be whipped at any time.

Does a slave look dissatisfied with his condition? It is said, that he has the devil in him, and it must be whipped out.

Does he answer loudly, when spoken to by his master, with an air of self-conscious-ness? Then, must he be taken down a button-hole lower, by the lash, well laid on.

Does he forget, and omit to pull off his hat, when approaching a white person? Then, he must, or may be, whipped for his bad manners.

Does he ever venture to vindicate his conduct, when harshly and unjustly accused? Then, he is guilty of impudence, one of the greatest crimes in the social catalogue of southern society.
To allow a slave to escape punishment, who has impudently attempted to exculpate himself from unjust charges, preferred against him by some white person, is to be guilty of great dereliction of duty.

Does a slave ever venture to suggest a better way of doing a thing, no matter what? He is, altogether, too officious—wise above what is written—and he deserves, even if he does not get, a flogging for his presumption.

Does he, while plowing, break a plow, or while hoeing, break a hoe, or while chopping, break an ax? No matter what were the imperfections of the implement broken, or the natural liabilities for breaking, the slave can be whipped for carelessness.

The reverend slaveholder could always find something of this sort, to justify him in using the lash several times during the week. But, to continue the thread of my story, through my experience when at Mr. William Freeland's.

My poor, weather-beaten bark now reached smoother water, and gentler breezes. My stormy life at Covey's had been of service to me. The things that would have seemed very hard, had I gone direct to Mr. Freeland's, from the home of Master Thomas, were now (after the hardships at Covey's) "trifles light as air." I was still a field hand, and had come to prefer the severe labor of the field, to the enervating duties of a house servant. I had become large and strong; and had begun to take pride in the fact, that I could do as much hard work as some of the older men. There is much rivalry among slaves, at times, as to which can do the most work, and masters generally seek to promote such rivalry. But some of us were too wise to race with each other very long. Such racing, we had the sagacity to see, was not likely to pay. We had our times for measuring each other's strength, but we knew too much to keep up the competition so long as to produce an extraordinary day's work. We knew that if, by extraordinary exertion, a large quantity of work was done in one day, the fact, becoming known to the master, might lead him to require the same amount every day. This thought was enough to bring us to a dead halt when over so much excited for the race.

At Mr. Freeland's, my condition was every way improved. I was no longer the poor scape-goat that I was when at Covey's, where every wrong thing done was saddled upon me, and where other slaves were whipped over my shoulders. Mr. Freeland was too just a man thus to impose upon me, or upon any one else.
It is quite usual to make one slave the object of especial abuse, and to beat him often, with a view to its effect

upon others, rather than with any expectation that the slave whipped will be improved by it, but the man with whom I now was, could descend to no such meanness and wickedness. Every man here was held individually responsible for his own conduct.

This was a vast improvement on the rule at Covey's. There, I was the general pack horse. Bill Smith was protected, by a positive prohibition made by his rich master, and the command of the rich slaveholder is LAW to the poor one; Hughes was favored, because of his relationship to Covey; and the hands hired temporarily, escaped flogging, except as they got it over my poor shoulders. Of course, this comparison refers to the time when Covey could whip me.

Mr. Freeland, like Mr. Covey, gave his hands enough to eat, but, unlike Mr. Covey, he gave them time to take their meals; he worked us hard during the day, but gave us the night for rest—another advantage to be set to the credit of the sinner, as against that of the saint. We were seldom in the field after dark in the evening, or before sunrise in the morning.

Notwithstanding the improved condition which was now mine, and the many advantages I had gained by my new home, and my new master, I was still restless and discontented. I was about as hard to please by a master, as a master is by slave. The freedom from bodily torture and unceasing labor, had given my mind an increased sensibility, and imparted to it greater activity. I was not yet exactly in right relations. Beat and cuff your slave, keep him hungry and spiritless, and he will follow the chain of his master like a dog; but, feed and clothe him well—work him moderately—surround him with physical comfort—and dreams of freedom intrude. Give him a bad master, and he aspires to a good master; give him a good master, and he wishes to become his own master. Such is human nature. Thus elevated, a little, at Freeland's, shoots from the tree of liberty began to put forth tender buds, and dim hopes of the future began to dawn.

At Mr. Freeland's, I found myself in congenial society. There were Henry Harris, John Harris, Handy Caldwell, and Sandy Jenkins.

Henry and John were brothers, and belonged to Mr. Freeland. They were both remarkably bright and intelligent, though neither of them could read. Now for mischief! I had not been long at Freeland's before I was up to my old tricks. I early began to address my companions on the subject of education, and the advantages of intelligence over ignorance, and, as far as I dared, I tried to show the agency of ignorance in keeping men in slavery. Webster's spelling book and the Columbian Orator were looked into again. As summer came on, and the long Sabbath days stretched themselves over our idleness, I became uneasy, and wanted a Sabbath school, in which to exercise my gifts, and to impart the little knowledge of letters which I possessed, to my brother slaves. A house was hardly necessary in the summer time; I could hold my school under the shade of an old oak tree, as well as anywhere else. The thing was, to get the scholars, and to have them thoroughly imbued with the desire to learn.

Two such boys were quickly secured, in Henry and John, and from them the contagion spread. I was not long bringing around me twenty or thirty young men, who enrolled themselves, gladly, in my Sabbath school, and were willing to meet me regularly, under the trees or elsewhere, for the purpose of learning to read. It was surprising with what ease they provided themselves with spelling books. These were mostly the cast off books of their young masters or mistresses. I taught, at first, on our own farm. All were impressed with the necessity of keeping the matter as private as possible, for the fate of the St. Michael's attempt was notorious, and fresh in the minds of all. Our pious masters, at St. Michael's, must not know that a few of their dusky brothers were learning to read the word of God, lest they should come down upon us with the lash and chain. We might have met to drink whisky, to wrestle, fight, and to do other unseemly things, with no fear of interruption from the saints or sinners of St. Michael's.

But, to meet for the purpose of improving the mind and heart, by learning to read the sacred scriptures, was esteemed a most dangerous nuisance, to be instantly stopped. The slaveholders of St. Michael's, like slaveholders elsewhere, would always prefer to see the slaves engaged in degrading sports, rather than to see them acting like moral and accountable beings.

Had any one asked a religious white man, in St. Michael's, twenty years ago, the names of three men in that town, whose lives were most after the pattern of our Lord and Master, Jesus Christ, the first three would have been as follows:
GARRISON WEST, Class Leader.
WRIGHT FAIRBANKS, Class Leader.
THOMAS AULD, Class Leader.

And yet, these were men who ferociously rushed in upon my Sabbath school, at St. Michael's, armed with mob-like missiles. The plea for this outrage was then, as it is now and at all times—the danger to good order. If the slaves learnt to read, they would learn something else, and something worse. The peace of slavery would be disturbed; slave rule would be endangered.

After getting the school cleverly into operation, the second time holding it in the woods, behind the barn, and in the shade of trees—I succeeded in inducing a free colored man, who lived several miles from our house, to permit me to hold my school in a room at his house. He, very kindly, gave me this liberty; but he incurred much peril in doing so, for the assemblage was an unlawful one. I shall not mention, here, the name of this man; for it might, even now, subject him to persecution, al- though the offenses were committed more than twenty years ago. I had, at one time, more than forty scholars, all of the right sort; and many of them succeeded in learning to read. I have met several slaves from Maryland, who were once my scholars; and who obtained their freedom, I doubt not, partly in consequence of the ideas imparted to them in that school.

I have had various employments during my short life; but I look back to none with more satisfaction, than to that afforded by my Sunday school. An attachment, deep and lasting, sprung up between me and my persecuted pupils, which made parting from them intensely grievous; and, when I think that most of these dear souls are yet shut up in this abject thralldom, I am overwhelmed with grief.

Besides my Sunday school, I devoted three evenings a week to my fellow slaves, during the winter. Let the reader reflect upon the fact, that, in this christian country, men and women are hiding from professors of religion, in barns, in the woods and fields, in order to learn to read the holy bible. Those dear souls, who came to my Sabbath school, came not because it was popular or reputable to attend such a place, for they came under the liability of having forty stripes laid on their naked backs. Every moment they spend in my school, they were under this terrible liability; and, in this respect, I was sharer with them. Their minds had been cramped and starved by their cruel masters; the light of education had been completely excluded; and their hard earnings had been taken to educate their master's children. I felt a delight in circumventing the tyrants, and in blessing the victims of their curses.

The year at Mr. Freeland's passed off very smoothly, to outward seeming. Not a blow was given me during the whole year. To the credit of Mr. Freeland—irreligious though he was—it must be stated, that he was the best master I ever had, until I became my own master, and assumed for myself, as I had a right to do, the responsibility of my own existence and the exercise of my own powers. For much of the happiness—or absence of misery—with which I passed this year with Mr. Freeland, I am indebted to the genial temper and ardent friendship of my brother slaves. They were, every one of them, manly, generous and brave, yes; I say they were brave, and I will add, fine looking. It is seldom the lot of mortals to have truer and better friends than were the slaves on this farm. It is not uncommon to charge slaves with great treachery toward each other, and to believe them incapable of confiding in each other; but I must say, that I never loved, esteemed, or confided in men, more than I did in these. They were as true as steel, and no band of brothers could have been more loving. There were no mean advantages taken of each other, as is sometimes the case where slaves are situated as we were; no tattling; no giving each other bad names; and no elevating one at the expense of the other. We never undertook to do anything, of any importance, which was likely to affect each other, without mutual consultation. We were generally a unit, and moved together. Thoughts and sentiments were exchanged between us, which might well be called very incendiary, by oppressors and tyrants; and perhaps the time has not even now come, when it is safe to unfold all the flying suggestions which arise in the minds of intelligent slaves. Several of my friends and brothers, if yet alive, are still in some part of the house of bondage; and though twenty years have passed away, the suspicious malice of slavery might punish them for even listening to my thoughts.

The year is ended, and we are now in the midst of the Christmas holidays, which are kept this year as last, according to the general description previously given.

19

The Run-Away Plot

I am now at the beginning of the year 1836, a time favorable for serious thoughts. The mind naturally occupies itself with the mysteries of life in all its phases —the ideal, the real and the actual. Sober people look both ways at the beginning of the year, surveying the errors of the past, and providing against possible errors of the future. I, too, was thus exercised. "Notwithstanding," thought I, "the many resolutions and prayers I have made, in behalf of freedom, I am, this first day of the year 1836, still a slave, still wandering in the depths of spirit-devouring thralldom.

At the close of the year 1835, Mr. Freeland, my temporary master, had bought me of Capt. Thomas Auld, for the year 1836. His promptness in securing my services, would have been flattering to my vanity, had I been ambitious to win the reputation of being a valuable slave. Even as it was, I felt a slight degree of complacency at the circumstance. It showed he was as well pleased with me as a slave, as I was with him as a master.

But the kindness of the slavemaster only gilds the chain of slavery, and detracts nothing from its weight or power. The thought that men are made for other and better uses than slavery, thrives best under the gentle treatment of a kind master. But the grim visage of slavery can assume no smiles which can fascinate the partially enlightened slave, into a forgetfulness of his bondage, nor of the desirableness of liberty.

I was not through the first month of this, my second year with the kind and gentlemanly Mr. Freeland, before I was earnestly considering and advising plans for gaining that freedom, which, when I was but a mere child, I had ascertained to be the natural and inborn right of every member of the human family. The desire for this freedom had been benumbed, while I was under the brutalizing dominion of Covey; and it had been postponed, and rendered inoperative, by my truly pleasant Sunday school engagements with my friends, during the year 1835. It had, however, never entirely subsided. I hated slavery, always, and the desire for freedom only needed a favorable breeze, to fan it into a blaze, at any moment.
The thought of only being a creature of the present and the past, troubled me, and I longed to have a future—a

future with hope in it. The dawning of this, another year, awakened me from my temporary slumber, and roused into life my latent, but long cherished aspirations for freedom. I was now not only ashamed to be contented in slavery, but ashamed to seem to be contented. The intense desires, now felt, to be free, quickened by my present favorable circumstances, brought me to the determination to act, as well as to think and speak. Accordingly, at the beginning of this year 1836, I took upon me a solemn vow, that the year which had now dawned upon me should not close, without witnessing an earnest attempt, on my part, to gain my liberty. This vow only bound me to make my escape individually; but the year spent with Mr. Freeland had attached me, as with "hooks of steel," to my brother slaves. The most affectionate and confiding friendship existed between us; and I felt it my duty to give them an opportunity to share in my virtuous determination by frankly disclosing to them my plans and purposes.

Toward Henry and John Harris, I felt a friendship as strong as one man can feel for another; for I could have died with and for them. To them, therefore, with a suitable degree of caution, I began to disclose my sentiments and plans; sounding them, the while on the subject of running away, provided a good chance should offer. I scarcely need tell the reader, that I did my very best to imbue the minds of my dear friends with my own views and feelings. Thoroughly awakened, now, and with a definite vow upon me, all my little reading, which had any bearing on the subject of human rights, was rendered available in my communications with my friends. That (to me) gem of a book, the Columbian Orator, with its eloquent orations and spicy dialogues, denouncing oppression and slavery—telling of what had been dared, done and suffered by men, to obtain the inestimable boon of liberty—was still fresh in my memory, and whirled into the ranks of my speech with the aptitude of well trained soldiers, going through the drill. The fact is, I here began my public speaking. I canvassed, with Henry and John, the subject of slavery, and dashed against it the condemning brand of God's eternal justice, which it every hour violates. My fellow servants were neither indifferent, dull, nor inapt. Our feelings were more alike than our opinions. All, however, were ready to act, when a feasible plan should be proposed. "Show us how the thing is to be done," said they, "and all is clear."

But here came a new trouble. Thoughts and purposes so incendiary as those I now cherished, could not agitate the mind long, without danger of making themselves manifest to scrutinizing and unfriendly beholders. I had reason to fear that my sable face might prove altogether too transparent for the safe concealment of my hazardous enterprise. Plans of greater moment have leaked through stone walls, and revealed their projectors. But, here was no stone wall to hide my purpose. I would have given my poor, tell tale face for the immoveable countenance of an Indian, for it was far from being proof against the daily, searching glances of those with whom I met.

It is the interest and business of slaveholders to study human nature, with a view to practical results, and many of them attain astonishing proficiency in discerning the thoughts and emotions of slaves. They have to deal not with earth, wood, or stone, but with men; and, by every regard they have for their safety and prosperity, they must study to know the material on which they are at work. So much intellect as the slaveholder has around him, requires watching. Their safety depends upon their vigilance. Conscious of the injustice and wrong they are every hour perpetrating, and knowing what they themselves would do if made the victims of such wrongs, they are looking out for the first signs of the dread retribution of justice. They watch, therefore, with skilled and practiced eyes, and have learned to read, with great accuracy, the state of mind and heart of the slaves, through his sable face.

Often relying on their superior position and wisdom, they hector and torture the slave into a confession, by affecting to know the truth of their accusations. "You have got the devil in you," say they, "and we will whip him out of you." I have often been put thus to the torture, on bare suspicion. This system has its disadvantages as well as their opposite. The slave is sometimes whipped into the confession of offenses which he never committed. The reader will see that the good old rule—"a man is to be held innocent until proved to be guilty"—does not hold good on the slave plantation. Suspicion and torture are the approved methods of getting at the truth, here. It was necessary for me, therefore, to keep a watch over my deportment, lest the enemy should get the better of me.

But with all our caution and studied reserve, I am not sure that Mr. Freeland did not suspect that all was not right with us. It did seem that he watched us more narrowly, after the plan of escape had been conceived and discussed amongst us. Men seldom see themselves as others see them; and while, to ourselves, everything connected with our contemplated escape appeared concealed, Mr. Freeland may have, with the peculiar prescience of a slaveholder, mastered the huge thought which was disturbing our peace in slavery.

I am the more inclined to think that he suspected us, because, prudent as we were, as I now look back, I can see that we did many silly things, very well calculated to awaken suspicion. We were, at times, remarkably buoyant, singing hymns and making joyous exclamations, almost as triumphant in their tone as if we reached a land of freedom and safety. A keen observer might have detected in our repeated singing of

    O Canaan, sweet Canaan,
    I am bound for the land of Canaan,

something more than a hope of reaching heaven. We meant to reach the north—and the north was our Canaan.

> I thought I heard them say,
> There were lions in the way,
> I don't expect to Star
>   Much longer here.
> Run to Jesus—shun the danger—
> I don't expect to stay
>   Much longer here.

was a favorite air, and had a double meaning. In the lips of some, it meant the expectation of a speedy summons to a world of spirits; but, in the lips of our company, it simply meant, a speedy pilgrimage toward a free state, and deliverance from all the evils and dangers of slavery.

I had succeeded in winning to my (what slaveholders would call wicked) scheme, a company of five young men, the very flower of the neighborhood, each one of whom would have commanded one thousand dollars in the home market. At New Orleans, they would have brought fifteen hundred dollars a piece, and, perhaps, more. The names of our party were as follows: Henry Harris; John Harris, brother to Henry; Sandy Jenkins, the one who gave me the root back when I was under Covey; Charles Roberts, and Henry Bailey. I was the youngest, but one, of the party. I had, however, the advantage of them all, in experience, and in a knowledge of letters. This gave me great influence over them. Perhaps not one of them, left to himself, would have dreamed of escape as a possible thing. Not one of them was self-moved in the matter. They all wanted to be free; but the serious thought of running away, had not entered into their minds, until I won them to the undertaking. They all were tolerably well off—for slaves—and had dim hopes of being set free, some day, by their masters. If anyone is to blame for disturbing the quiet of the slaves and slavemasters of the neighborhood of St. Michael's, I am the man. I claim to be the instigator of the high crime (as the slaveholders regard it) and I kept life in it, until life could be kept in it no longer.

Pending the time of our contemplated departure out of our Egypt, we met often by night, and on every Sunday. At these meetings we talked the matter over; told our hopes and fears, and the difficulties discovered or imagined; and, like men of sense, we counted the cost of the enterprise to which we were committing ourselves.

These meetings must have resembled, on a small scale, the meetings of revolutionary conspirators, in their primary condition. We were plotting against our (so called) lawful rulers; with this difference that we sought our own good, and not the harm of our enemies. We did not seek to overthrow them, but to escape from them. As for Mr. Freeland, we all liked him, and would have gladly remained with him, as freeman. LIBERTY was our aim; and we had now come to think that we had a right to liberty, against every obstacle even against the lives of our enslavers.

We had several words, expressive of things, important to us, which we understood, but which, even if distinctly heard by an outsider, would convey no certain meaning. I have reasons for suppressing these passwords, which the reader will easily divine. I hated the secrecy; but where slavery is powerful, and liberty is weak, the latter is driven to concealment or to destruction.

The prospect was not always a bright one. At times, we were almost tempted to abandon the enterprise, and to get back to that comparative peace of mind, which even a man under the gallows might feel, when all hope of escape had vanished. Quiet bondage was felt to be better than the doubts, fears and uncertainties, which now so sadly perplexed and disturbed us.

The infirmities of humanity, generally, were represented in our little band. We were confident, bold and determined, at times; and, again, doubting, timid and wavering; whistling, like the boy in the graveyard, to keep away the spirits.

To look at the map, and observe the proximity of Eastern Shore, Maryland, to Delaware and Pennsylvania, it may seem to the reader quite absurd, to regard the proposed escape as a formidable undertaking. The real distance was great enough, but the imagined distance was, to our ignorance, even greater. Every slaveholder seeks to impress his slave with a belief in the boundlessness of slave territory, and of his own almost illimitable power. We all had vague and indistinct notions of the geography of the country.

The distance, however, is not the chief trouble. The nearer are the lines of a slave state and the borders of a free one, the greater the peril. Hired kidnappers infest these borders. Then, too, we knew that merely reaching a free state did not free us; that, wherever caught, we could be returned to slavery. We could see no spot on this side the ocean, where we could be free. We had heard of Canada, the real Canaan of the American bondmen, simply as a country to which the wild goose and the swan repaired at the end of winter, to escape the heat of summer, but not as the home of man. I knew something of theology, but nothing of geography. I really did not, at that time, know that there was a state of New York, or a state of Massachusetts. I had heard of Pennsylvania, Delaware and New Jersey, and all the southern states, but was ignorant of the free states, generally. New York city was our northern limit, and to go there, and be forever harassed with the liability of being hunted down and returned to slavery—with the certainty of being treated ten times worse than we had ever been treated before was a prospect far from delightful, and it might well cause some hesitation about engaging in the enterprise.

The case, sometimes, to our excited visions, stood thus: At every gate through which we had to pass, we saw a watchman; at every ferry, a guard; on every bridge, a sentinel; and in every wood, a patrol or slave-hunter. We were hemmed in on every side. The good to be sought, and the evil to be shunned, were flung in the balance, and weighed against each other. On the one hand, there stood slavery; a stern reality, glaring frightfully upon us, with the blood of millions in his polluted skirts—terrible to behold—greedily devouring our hard earnings and feeding himself upon our flesh. Here was the evil from which to escape. On the other hand, far away, back in the hazy distance, where all forms seemed but shadows, under the flickering light of the north star—behind some craggy hill or snow-covered mountain—stood a doubtful freedom, half frozen, beckoning us to her icy domain. This was the good to be sought. The inequality was as great as that between certainty and uncertainty. This, in itself, was enough to stagger us; but when we came to survey the untrodden road, and conjecture the many possible difficulties, we were appalled, and at times, as I have said, were upon the point of giving over the struggle altogether.

The reader can have little idea of the phantoms of trouble which flit, in such circumstances, before the uneducated mind of the slave. Upon either side, we saw grim death assuming a variety of horrid shapes. Now, it was starvation, causing us, in a strange and friendless land, to eat our own flesh. Now, we were contending with the waves (for our journey was in part by water) and were drowned. Now, we were hunted by dogs, and overtaken and torn to pieces by their merciless fangs. We were stung by scorpions—chased by wild beasts—bitten by snakes; and, worst of all, after having succeeded in swimming rivers—encountering wild beasts—sleeping in the woods—suffering hunger, cold, heat and nakedness—we supposed ourselves to be overtaken by hired kidnappers, who, in the name of the law, and for their thrice accursed reward, would, perchance, fire upon us—kill some, wound others, and capture all. This dark picture, drawn by ignorance and fear, at times greatly shook our determination, and not infrequently caused us to rather bear those ills we had than fly to others which we knew not of.

No man can tell the intense agony which is felt by the slave, when wavering on the point of making his escape. All that he has is at stake; and even that which he has not, is at stake, also. The life which he has, may be lost, and the liberty which he seeks, may not be gained.

Patrick Henry, to a listening senate, thrilled by his magic eloquence, and ready to stand by him in his boldest flights, could say, GIVE ME LIBERTY OR GIVE ME DEATH, and this saying was a sublime one, even for a freeman; but, incomparably more sublime, is the same sentiment, when practically asserted by men accustomed to the lash and chain—men whose sensibilities must have become more or less deadened by their bondage. With us it was a doubtful liberty, at best, that we sought; and a certain, lingering death in the rice swamps and sugar fields, if we failed.

Life is not lightly regarded by men of sane minds. It is precious, alike to the pauper and to the prince—to the slave, and to his master; and yet, I believe there was not one among us, who would not rather have been shot down, than pass away life in hopeless bondage.

In the progress of our preparations, Sandy, the root man, became troubled. He began to have dreams, and some of them were very distressing. One of these, which happened on a Friday night, was, to him, of great significance; and I am quite ready to confess, that I felt somewhat damped by it myself. He said, "I dreamed, last night, that I was roused from sleep, by strange noises, like the voices of a swarm of angry birds, that caused a roar as they passed, which fell upon my ear like a coming gale over the tops of the trees. Looking up to see what it could mean," said Sandy, "I saw you, Frederick, in the claws of a huge bird, surrounded by a large number of birds, of all colors and sizes. These were all picking at you, while you, with your arms, seemed to be trying to protect your eyes. Passing over me, the birds flew in a south-westerly direction, and I watched them until they were clean out of sight. Now, I saw this as plainly as I now see you."

I confess I did not like this dream; but I threw off concern about it, by attributing it to the general excitement and perturbation consequent upon our contemplated plan of escape. I could not, however, shake off its effect at once. I felt that it boded me no good. Sandy was unusually emphatic and oracular, and his manner had much to do with the impression made upon me.

The plan of escape which I recommended, and to which my comrades assented, was to take a large canoe, owned by Mr. Hamilton, and, on the Saturday night previous to the Easter holidays, launch out into the Chesapeake bay, and paddle for its head—a distance of seventy miles with all our might. Our course, on reaching this point, was, to turn the canoe adrift, and bend our steps toward the north star, till we reached a free state.

There were several objections to this plan. One was, the danger from gales on the bay. In rough weather, the waters of the Chesapeake are much agitated, and there is danger, in a canoe, of being swamped by the waves. Another objection was, that the canoe would soon be missed; the absent persons would, at once, be suspected of having taken it; and we should be pursued by some of the fast sailing bay craft out of St. Michael's. Then, again, if we reached the head of the bay, and turned the canoe adrift, she might prove a guide to our track, and bring the land hunters after us.

These and other objections were set aside, by the stronger ones which could be urged against every other plan that could then be suggested. On the water, we had a chance of being regarded as fishermen, in the service of a master. On the other hand, by taking the land route, through the counties adjoining Delaware, we should be subjected to all manner of interruptions, and many very disagreeable questions, which might give us serious trouble. Any white man is authorized to stop a man of color, on any road, and examine him, and arrest him, if he so desires.

By this arrangement, many abuses occur. Cases have been known, where freemen have been called upon to show their free papers, by a pack of ruffians—and, on the presentation of the papers, the ruffians have torn them up, and seized their victim, and sold him to a life of endless bondage.

The week before our intended start, I wrote a pass for each of our party, giving them permission to visit Baltimore, during the Easter holidays. The pass ran after this manner:

This is to certify, that I, the undersigned, have given the bearer, my servant, John, full liberty to go to Baltimore, to spend the Easter holidays.

W.H.
Near St. Michael's, Talbot county, Maryland

Although we were not going to Baltimore, and were intending to land east of North Point, in the direction where I had seen the Philadelphia steamers go, these passes might be made useful to us in the lower part of the bay, while steering toward Baltimore. These were not, however, to be shown by us, until all other answers failed to satisfy the inquirer. We were all fully alive to the importance of being calm and self-possessed, when accosted, if accosted we should be; and we more times than one rehearsed to each other how we should behave in the hour of trial.

These were long, tedious days and nights. The suspense was painful, in the extreme. To balance probabilities, where life and liberty hang on the result, requires steady nerves. I panted for action, and was glad when the day, at the close of which we
were to start, dawned upon us. Sleeping, the night before, was out of the question. I probably felt more deeply than any of my companions, because I was the instigator of the movement. The responsibility of the whole enterprise rested on my shoulders. The glory of success, and the shame and confusion of failure, could not be matters of indifference to me. Our food was prepared; our clothes were packed up; we were all ready to go, and impatient for Saturday morning—considering that the last morning of our bondage.

I cannot describe the tempest and tumult of my brain that morning. The reader will please to bear in mind, that, in a slave state, an unsuccessful runaway is not only subjected to cruel torture, and sold away to the far south, but he is frequently execrated by the other slaves. He is charged with making the condition of the other slaves intolerable, by laying them all under the suspicion of their masters—subjecting them to greater vigilance, and imposing greater limitations on their privileges. I dreaded murmurs from this quarter. It is difficult, too, for a slavemaster to believe that slaves escaping have not been aided in their flight by someone of their fellow slaves. When, therefore, a slave is missing, every slave on the place is closely examined as to his knowledge of the undertaking; and they are sometimes even tortured, to make them disclose what they are suspected of knowing of such escape.

Our anxiety grew more and more intense, as the time of our intended departure for the north drew nigh. It was truly felt to be a matter of life and death with us; and we fully intended to fight as well as run, if necessity should occur for that extremity. But the trial hour was not yet to come. It was easy to resolve, but not so easy to act. I expected there might be some drawing back, at the last. It was natural that there should be; therefore, during the intervening time, I lost no opportunity to explain away difficulties, to remove doubts, to dispel fears, and to inspire all with firmness. It was too late to look back; and now was the time to go forward. Like most other men, we had done the talking part of our work, long and well; and the time had come to act as if we were in earnest, and meant to be as true in action as in words. I did not forget to appeal to the pride of my comrades, by telling them that, if after having solemnly promised to go, as they had done, they now failed to make the attempt, they would, in effect, brand themselves with cowardice, and might as well sit down, fold their arms, and ac- knowledge themselves as fit only to be slaves. This detestable character, all were unwilling to assume. Every man except Sandy (he, much to our regret, withdrew) stood firm; and at our last meeting we pledged ourselves afresh, and in the most solemn manner, that, at the time appointed, we would certainly start on our long journey for a free country. This meeting was in the middle of the week, at the end of which we were to start.

Early that morning we went, as usual, to the field, but with hearts that beat quickly and anxiously. Any one intimately acquainted with us, might have seen that all was not well with us, and that some monster lingered in our thoughts. Our work that morning was the same as it had been for several days past—drawing out and spreading manure. While thus engaged, I had a sudden presentiment, which flashed upon me like lightning in a dark night, revealing to the lonely traveler the gulf before, and the enemy behind. I instantly turned to Sandy Jenkins, who was near me, and said to him, "Sandy, we are betrayed; something has just told me so." I felt as sure of it, as if the officers were there in sight. Sandy said, "Man, dat is strange; but I feel just as you do." If my mother—then long in her grave—had appeared before me, and told me that we were betrayed, I could not, at that moment, have felt more certain of the fact.

In a few minutes after this, the long, low and distant notes of the horn summoned us from the field to breakfast. I felt as one may be supposed to feel before being led forth to be executed for some great offense. I wanted no breakfast; but I went with the other slaves toward the house, for form's sake. My feelings were not disturbed as to the right of running away; on that point I had no trouble, whatever. My anxiety arose from a sense of the consequences of failure.

In thirty minutes after that vivid presentiment came the apprehended crash. On reaching the house, for breakfast, and glancing my eye toward the lane gate, the worst was at once made known. The lane gate off Mr. Freeland's house is nearly a half mile from the door, and shaded by the heavy wood which bordered the main road. I was, however, able to descry four white men, and two colored men, approaching. The white men were on horseback, and the colored men were walking behind, and seemed to be tied. "It is all over with us," thought I, "we are surely betrayed." I now became composed, or at least comparatively so, and calmly awaited the result. I watched the ill-omened company, till I saw them enter the gate. Successful flight was impossible, and I made up my mind to stand, and meet the evil, whatever it might be; for I was not without a slight hope that things might turn differently from what I at first expected.

In a few moments, in came Mr. William Hamilton, riding very rapidly, and evidently much excited. He was in the habit of riding very slowly, and was seldom known to gallop his horse. This time, his horse was nearly at full speed, causing the dust to roll thick behind him. Mr. Hamilton, though one of the most resolute men in the whole neighborhood, was, nevertheless, a remarkably mild spoken man; and, even when greatly excited, his language was cool and circumspect. He came to the door, and inquired if Mr. Freeland was in. I told him that Mr. Freeland was at the barn. Off the old gentleman rode toward the barn, with unwonted speed. Mary, the cook, was at a loss to know what was the matter, and I did not profess any skill in making her understand. I knew she would have united, as readily as anyone, in cursing me for bringing trouble into the family; so I held my peace, leaving matters to develop themselves, without my assistance. In a few moments, Mr. Hamilton and Mr. Freeland came down from the barn to the house; and, just as they made their appearance in the front yard, three men (who proved to be constables) came dashing into the lane, on horseback, as if summoned by a sign requiring quick work. A few seconds brought them into the front yard, where they hastily dismounted, and tied their horses. This done, they joined Mr. Freeland and Mr. Hamilton, who were standing a short distance from the kitchen. A few moments were spent, as if in consulting how to proceed, and then the whole party walked up to the kitchen door. There was now no one in the kitchen but myself and John Harris. Henry and Sandy were yet at the barn. Mr. Freeland came inside the kitchen door, and with an agitated voice, called me by name, and told me to come forward; that there was some gentlemen who wished to see me. I stepped toward them, at the door, and asked what they wanted, when the constables grabbed me, and told me that I had better not resist; that I had been in a scrape, or was said to have been in one; that they were merely going to take me where I could be examined; that they were going to carry me to St. Michael's, to have me brought before my master. They further said, that, in case the evidence against me was not true, I should be acquitted.

I was now firmly tied, and completely at the mercy of my captors. Resistance was idle. They were five in number, armed to the very teeth. When they had secured me, they next turned to John Harris, and, in a few moments, succeeded in tying him as firmly as they had already tied me. They next turned toward Henry Harris, who had now returned from the barn. "Cross your hands," said the constables to Henry. "I won't" said Henry, in a voice so firm and clear, and in a manner so determined, as for a moment to arrest all proceedings. "Won't you cross your hands?" said Tom Graham, the constable. "No I won't," said Henry, with increasing emphasis. Mr. Hamilton, Mr. Freeland, and the officers, now came near to Henry. Two of the constables drew out their shining pistols, and swore by the name of God, that he should cross his hands, or they would shoot him down. Each of these hired ruffians now cocked their pistols, and, with fingers apparently on the triggers, presented their deadly weapons to the breast of the unarmed slave, saying, at the same time, if he did not cross his hands, they would "blow his d—d heart out of him."

"Shoot! shoot me!" said Henry. "You can't kill me but once. Shoot!—shoot! and be d—d. I won't be tied." This, the brave fellow said in a voice as defiant and heroic in its tone, as was the language itself; and, at the moment of saying this, with the pistols at his very breast, he quickly raised his arms, and dashed them from the puny hands of his assassins, the weapons flying in opposite directions. Now came the struggle. All hands was now rushed upon the brave fellow, and, after beating him for some time, they succeeded in overpowering and tying him. Henry put me to shame; he fought, and fought bravely. John and I had made no resistance.

The fact is, I never see much use in fighting, unless there is a reasonable probability of whipping somebody. Yet there was something almost providential in the resistance made by the gallant Henry. But for that resistance, every soul of us would have been hurried off to the far south. Just a moment previous to the trouble with Henry, Mr. Hamilton mildly said—and this gave me the unmistakable clue to the cause of our arrest—"Perhaps we had now better make a search for those protections, which we understand Frederick has written for himself and the rest." Had these passes been found, they would have been point blank proof against us, and would have confirmed all the statements of our betrayer. Thanks to the resistance of Henry, the excitement produced by the scuffle drew all attention in that direction, and I succeeded in flinging my pass, unobserved, into the fire. The confusion attendant upon the scuffle, and the apprehension of further trouble, perhaps, led our captors to forego, for the present, any search for "those protections" which Frederick was said to have written for his companions; so we were not yet convicted of the purpose to run away; and it was evident that there was some doubt, on the part of all, whether we had been guilty of such a purpose.

Just as we were all completely tied, and about ready to start toward St. Michael's, and thence to jail, Mrs. Betsey Freeland (mother to William, who was very much attached—after the southern fashion—to Henry and John, they having been reared from childhood in her house) came to the kitchen door, with her hands full of biscuits—for we had not had time to take our breakfast that morning—and divided them between Henry and John. This done, the lady made the following parting address to me, looking and pointing her bony finger at me. "You devil! you yellow devil! It was you that put it into the heads of Henry and John to run away. But for you, you long legged yellow devil, Henry and John would never have thought of running away." I gave the lady a look, which called forth a scream of mingled wrath and terror, as she slammed the kitchen door, and went in, leaving me, with the rest, in hands as harsh as her own broken voice.

Could the kind reader have been quietly riding along the main road to or from Easton that morning, his eye would have met a painful sight. He would have seen five young men, guilty of no crime, save that of preferring liberty to a life of bondage, drawn along the public highway—firmly bound together—tramping through dust and heat, barefooted and bareheaded—fastened to three strong horses, whose riders were armed to the teeth, with pistols and daggers—on their way to prison, like felons, and suffering every possible insult from the crowds of idle, vulgar people, who clustered around, and heartlessly made their failure the occasion for all manner of ribaldry and sport.

As I looked upon this crowd of vile persons, and saw myself and friends thus assailed and persecuted, I could not help seeing the fulfillment of Sandy's dream. I was in the hands of moral vultures, and firmly held in their sharp talons, and was hurried away toward Easton, in a southeasterly direction, amid the jeers of new birds of the same feather, through every neighborhood we passed. It seemed to me (and this shows the good understanding between the slaveholders and their allies) that everybody we met knew the cause of our arrest, and were out, awaiting our passing by, to feast their vindictive eyes on our misery and to gloat over our ruin. Some said I ought to be hanged, and others, I ought to be burnt, others, I ought to have the "hide" taken from my back; while no one gave us a kind word or sympathizing look, except the poor slaves, who were lifting their heavy hoes, and who cautiously glanced at us through the post-and-rail fences, behind which they were at work.

Our sufferings, that morning, can be more easily imagined than described. Our hopes were all blasted, at a blow. The cruel injustice, the victorious crime, and the helplessness of innocence, led me to ask, in my ignorance and weakness "Where now is the God of justice and mercy? And why have these wicked men the power thus to trample upon our rights, and to insult our feelings?" And yet, in the next moment came the consoling thought, "The day of oppressor will come at last." Of one thing I could be glad—not one of my dear friends, upon whom I had brought this great calamity, either by word or look, reproached me for having led them into it. We were a band of brothers, and never dearer to each other than now. The thought which gave us the most pain was the probable separation which would now take place, in case we were sold off to the far south, as we were likely to be. While the constables were looking forward, Henry and I, being fastened together, could occasionally exchange a word, without being observed by the kidnappers who had us in charge.

"What shall I do with my pass?" said Henry. "Eat it with your biscuit," said I; "it won't do to tear it up."

We were now near St. Michael's. The direction concerning the passes was passed around, and executed. "Own nothing!" said I. "Own nothing!" was passed around and enjoined, and assented to. Our confidence in each other was unshaken; and we were quite resolved to succeed or fail together—as much after the calamity which had befallen us, as before.

On reaching St. Michael's, we underwent a sort of examination at my master's store, and it was evident to my mind, that Master Thomas suspected the truthfulness of the evidence upon which they had acted in arresting us; and that he only affected, to some extent, the positiveness with which he asserted our guilt. There was nothing said by any of our company, which could, in any manner, prejudice our cause; and there was hope, yet, that we should be able to return to our homes—if for nothing else, at least to find out the guilty man or woman who had betrayed us.

To this end, we all denied that we had been guilty of intended flight. Master Thomas said that the evidence he had of our intention to run away, was strong enough to hang us, in a case of murder. "But," said I, "the cases are not equal. If murder were committed, some one must have committed it—the thing is done! In our case, nothing has been done! We have not run away. Where is the evidence against us? We were quietly at our work."

I talked thus, with unusual freedom, to bring out the evidence against us, for we all wanted, above all things, to know the guilty wretch who had betrayed us, that we might have something tangible upon which to pour the execrations. From something which dropped, in the course of the talk, it appeared that there was but one witness against us—and that that witness could not be produced. Master Thomas would not tell us who his informant was; but we suspected, and suspected one person only. Several circumstances seemed to point SANDY out, as our betrayer. His entire knowledge of our plans his participation in them—his withdrawal from us—his dream, and his simultaneous presentiment that we were betrayed—the taking us, and the leaving him—were calculated to turn suspicion toward him; and yet, we could not suspect him. We all loved him too well to think it possible that he could have betrayed us. So we rolled the guilt on other shoulders.

We were literally dragged, that morning, behind horses, a distance of fifteen miles, and placed in the Easton jail. We were glad to reach the end of our journey, for our pathway had been the scene of insult and mortification.

Such is the power of pub- lic opinion, that it is hard, even for the innocent, to feel the happy consolations of innocence, when they fall under the maledictions of this power. How could we regard ourselves as in the right, when all about us denounced us as criminals, and had the power and the disposition to treat us as such.

In jail, we were placed under the care of Mr. Joseph Graham, the sheriff of the county. Henry, and John, and myself, were placed in one room, and Henry Baily and Charles Roberts, in another, by themselves. This separation was intended to deprive us of the advantage of concert, and to prevent trouble in jail.

Once shut up, a new set of tormentors came upon us. A swarm of imps, in human shape the slave traders, deputy slave traders, and agents of slave traders—that gather in every country town of the state, watching for chances to buy human flesh, flocked in upon us, to ascertain if our masters had placed us in jail to be sold. Such a set of debased and villainous creatures, I never saw before, and hope never to see again. I felt myself surrounded as by a pack of fiends, fresh from perdition. They laughed, leered, and grinned at us; saying, "Ah! boys, we've got you, haven't we? So you were about to make your escape? Where were you going to?" After taunting us, and peering at us, as long as they liked, they one by one subjected us to an examination, with a view to ascertain our value; feeling our arms and legs, and shaking us by the shoulders to see if we were sound and healthy; impudently asking us, "how we would like to have them for masters?" To such questions, we were, very much to their annoyance, quite dumb, disdaining to answer them. For one, I detested the whisky-bloated gamblers in human flesh; and I believe I was as much detested by them in turn. One fellow told me, "if he had me, he would cut the devil out of me pretty quick."

These Negro buyers are very offensive to the genteel southern Christian public. They are looked upon, in respectable Maryland society, as necessary, but detestable characters. Yes; they are a legitimate fruit of slavery; and it is a puzzle to make out a case of greater villainy for them, than for the slaveholders, who make such a class possible. They are mere hucksters of the surplus slave produce of Maryland and Virginia coarse, cruel, and swaggering bullies, whose very breathing is of blasphemy and blood.

Aside from these slave-buyers, who infested the prison from time to time, our quarters were much more comfortable than we had any right to expect they would be. Our allowance of food was small and coarse, but our room was the best in the jail—neat and spacious, and with nothing about it necessarily reminding us of being in prison, but its heavy locks and bolts and the black, iron lattice-work at the windows. We were prisoners of state, compared with most slaves who are put into that Easton jail. But the place was not one of contentment. Bolts, bars and grated windows are not acceptable to freedom-loving people of any color. The suspense, too, was painful. Every step on the stairway was listened to, in the hope that the comer would cast a ray of light on our fate. We would have given the hair off our heads for half a dozen words with one of the waiters in Sol. Lowe's hotel. Such waiters were in the way of hearing, at the table, the probable course of things. We could see them flitting about in their white jackets in front of this hotel, but could speak to none of them.

Soon after the holidays were over, contrary to all our expectations, Messrs. Hamilton and Freeland came up to Easton; not to make a bargain with the "Georgia traders," nor to send us up to Austin Woldfolk, as is usual in the case of run-away slaves, but to release Charles, Henry Harris, Henry Baily and John Harris, from prison, and this, too, without the infliction of a single blow. I was now left entirely alone in prison. The innocent had been taken, and the guilty left. My friends were separated from me, and apparently forever. This circumstance caused me more pain than any other incident connected with our capture and imprisonment. Thirty-nine lashes on my naked and bleeding back would have been joyfully borne, in preference to this separation from these, the friends of my youth. And yet, I could not but feel that I was the victim of something like justice. Why should these young men, who were led into this scheme by me, suffer as much as the instigator? I felt glad that they were leased from prison, and from the dread prospect of a life (or death I should rather say) in the rice swamps. It is due to the noble Henry, to say, that he seemed almost as reluctant to leave the prison with me in it, as he was to be tied and dragged to prison. But he and the rest knew that we should, in all the likelihoods of the case, be separated, in the event of being sold; and since we were now completely in the hands of our owners, we all concluded it would be best to go peaceably home.

Not until this last separation, dear reader, had I touched those profounder depths of desolation, which it is the lot of slaves often to reach. I was solitary in the world, and alone within the walls of a stone prison, left to a fate of life-long misery. I had hoped and expected much, for months before, but my hopes and expectations were now withered and blasted. The ever dreaded slave life in

Georgia, Louisiana and Alabama—from which escape is next to impossible now, stared me in the face. The possibility of ever becoming anything but an abject slave, a mere machine in the hands of an owner, had now fled, and it seemed to me it had fled forever. A life of living death, beset with the innumerable horrors of the cotton field, and the sugar plantation, seemed to be my doom. The fiends, who rushed into the prison when we were first put there, continued to visit me, and to ply me with questions and with their tantalizing remarks. I was insulted, but helpless; keenly alive to the demands of justice and liberty, but with no means of asserting them. To talk to those imps about justice and mercy, would have been as absurd as to reason with bears and tigers. Lead and steel are the only arguments that they understand.

After remaining in this life of misery and despair about a week, which, by the way, seemed a month, Master Thomas, very much to my surprise, and greatly to my relief, came to the prison, and took me out, for the purpose, as he said, of sending me to Alabama, with a friend of his, who would emancipate me at the end of eight years. I was glad enough to get out of prison; but I had no faith in the story that this friend of Capt. Auld would emancipate me, at the end of the time indicated. Besides, I never had heard of his having a friend in Alabama, and I took the announcement, simply as an easy and comfortable method of shipping me off to the far south. There was a little scandal, too, connected with the idea of one Christian selling another to the Georgia traders, while it was deemed every way proper for them to sell to others. I thought this friend in Alabama was an invention, to meet this difficulty, for Master Thomas was quite jealous of his Christian reputation, however unconcerned he might be about his real Christian character.

In these remarks, however, it is possible that I do Master Thomas Auld injustice. He certainly did not exhaust his power upon me, in the case, but acted, upon the whole, very generously, considering the nature of my offense. He had the power and the provocation to send me, without reserve, into the very everglades of Florida, beyond the remotest hope of emancipation; and his refusal to exercise that power, must be set down to his credit.

After lingering about St. Michael's a few days, and no friend from Alabama making his appearance to take me there, Master Thomas decided to send me back again to Baltimore, to live with his brother Hugh, with whom he was now at peace; possibly he became so by his profession of religion, at the camp-meeting in the Bay Side. Master Thomas told me that he wished me to go to Baltimore, and learn a trade; and that, if I behaved myself properly, he would emancipate me at twenty-five! Thanks for this one beam of hope in the future. The promise had but one fault; it seemed too good to be true.

20

Apprenticeship Life

Well! dear reader, I am not, as you may have already inferred, a loser by the general upstir, described in the foregoing chapter. The little domestic revolution, notwithstanding the sudden snub it got by the treachery of somebody—I dare not say or think who—did not, after all, end so disastrously, as when in the iron cage at Easton I conceived it would. The prospect, from that point, did look about as dark as any that ever cast its gloom over the vision of the anxious, out-looking, human spirit. "All is well that ends well." My affectionate comrades, Henry and John Harris are still with Mr. William Freeland. Charles Roberts and Henry Baily are safe at their homes. I have not, therefore, anything to regret on their account. Their masters have mercifully forgiven them, probably on the ground suggested in the spirited little speech of Mrs. Freeland, made to me just before leaving for the jail—namely: that they had been allured into the wicked scheme of making their escape, by me; and that, but for me, they would never have dreamed of a thing so shocking!

My friends had nothing to regret, either; for while they were watched more closely on account of what had happened, they were, doubtless, treated more kindly than before, and got new assurances that they would be legally emancipated, some day, provided their behavior should make them deserving, from that time forward. Not a blow, as I learned, was struck any one of them. As for Master William Freeland, good, unsuspecting soul, he did not believe that we were intending to run away at all. Having given—as he thought—no occasion to his boys to leave him, he could not think it probable that they had entertained a design so grievous.

This, however, was not the view taken of the matter by "Mas' Billy," as we used to call the soft spoken, but crafty and resolute Mr. William Hamilton. He had no doubt that the crime had been meditated; and regarding me as the instigator of it, he frankly told Master Thomas that he must remove me from that neighborhood, or he would shoot me down. He would not have one so dangerous as "Frederick" tampering with his slaves. William Hamilton was not a man whose threat might be safely disregarded. I have no doubt that he would have proved as good as his word, had the warning given not been promptly taken. He was furious at the thought of such a piece of high-handed theft, as we were about to perpetrate the stealing of our own bodies and souls! The feasibility of the plan, too, could the first steps have been taken, was marvelously plain. Besides, this was a new idea, this use of the bay. Slaves escaping, until now, had taken to the woods; they had never dreamed of profaning and abusing the waters of the noble Chesapeake, by making them the highway from slavery to freedom. Here was a broad road of destruction to slavery, which, before, had been looked upon as a wall of security by slaveholders.

But Master Billy could not get Mr. Freeland to see matters precisely as he did; nor could he get Master Thomas so excited as he was himself. The latter—I must say it to his credit—showed much humane feeling in his part of the transaction, and atoned for much that had been harsh, cruel and unreasonable in his former treatment of me and others. His clemency was quite unusual and unlooked for. "Cousin Tom" told me that while I was in jail, Master Thomas was very unhappy; and that the night before his going up to release me, he had walked the floor nearly all night, evincing great distress; that very tempting offers had been made to him by the Negro-traders, but he had rejected them all, saying that money could not tempt him to sell me to the far south. All this I can easily believe, for he seemed quite reluctant to send me away, at all. He told me that he only consented to do so, because of the very strong prejudice against me in the neighborhood, and that he feared for my safety if I remained there.

Thus, after three years spent in the country, roughing it in the field, and experiencing all sorts of hardships, I was again permitted to return to Baltimore, the very place, of all others, short of a free state, where I most desired to live. The three years spent in the country had made some difference in me, and in the household of Master Hugh.

"Little Tommy" was no longer little Tommy; and I was not the slender lad who had left for the Eastern Shore just three years before. The loving relations between me and Mas' Tommy were broken up. He was no longer dependent on me for protection, but felt himself a man, with other and more suitable associates. In childhood, he scarcely considered me inferior to himself certainly, as good as any other boy with whom he played; but the time had come when his friend must become his slave.

So we were cold, and we parted. It was a sad thing to me, that, loving each other as we had done, we must now take different roads. To him, a thousand avenues were open. Education had made him acquainted with all the treasures of the world, and liberty had flung open the gates thereunto; but I, who had attended him seven years, and had watched over him with the care of a big brother, fighting his battles in the street, and shielding him from harm, to an extent which had induced his mother to say, "Oh! Tommy is always safe, when he is with Freddy," must be confined to a single condition. He could grow, and become a MAN; I could grow, though I could not become a man, but must remain, all my life, a minor—a mere boy.

Thomas Auld, Junior, obtained a situation on board the brig "Tweed," and went to sea. I know not what has become of him; he certainly has my good wishes for his welfare and prosperity. There were few persons to whom I was more sincerely attached than to him, and there are few in the world I would be more pleased to meet.

Very soon after I went to Baltimore to live, Master Hugh succeeded in getting me hired to Mr. William Gardiner, an extensive ship builder on Fell's Point. I was placed here to learn to calk, a trade of which I already had some knowledge, gained while in Mr. Hugh Auld's shipyard, when he was a master builder. Gardiner's, however, proved a very unfavorable place for the accomplishment of that object. Mr. Gardiner was, that season, engaged in building two large man-of-war vessels, professedly for the Mexican government. These vessels were to be launched in the month of July of that year, and, in failure thereof, Mr. G. would forfeit a very considerable sum of money. So, when I entered the shipyard, all was hurry and driving. There were in the yard about one hundred men; of these about seventy or eighty were regular carpenters—privileged men. Speaking of my condition here I wrote, years ago—and I have now no reason to vary the picture as follows:

"There was no time to learn anything. Every man had to do that which he knew how to do. In entering the shipyard, my orders from Mr. Gardiner were, to do whatever the carpenters commanded me to do. This was placing me at the beck and call of about seventy-five men. I was to regard all these as masters. Their word was to be my law. My situation was a most trying one. At times I needed a dozen pair of hands. I was called a dozen ways in the space of a single minute. Three or four voices would strike my ear at the same moment. It was —"Fred, come help me to cant this timber here." "Fred, come carry this timber yonder."—"Fred, bring that roller here."—"Fred, go get a fresh can of water."—"Fred, come help saw off the end of this timber."—"Fred, go quick and get the crow bar."—"Fred, hold on the end of this fall."—"Fred, go to the blacksmith's shop, and get a new punch."— "Hurra, Fred! run and bring me a cold chisel."—"I say, Fred, bear a hand, and get up a fire as quick as lightning under that steam-box."—"Halloo, nigger! come, turn this grind-stone."—"Come, come! move, move! and bowse this timber forward."—"I say, darkey, blast your eyes, why don't you heat up some pitch?"—"Halloo! halloo! halloo!" (Three voices at the same time.) "Come here!—Go there!—Hold on where you are! D—n you, if you move, I'll knock your brains out!"

Such, dear reader, is a glance at the school which was mine, during, the first eight months of my stay at Baltimore. At the end of the eight months, Master Hugh refused longer to allow me to remain with Mr. Gardiner. The circumstance which led to his taking me away was a brutal outrage, committed upon me by the white apprentices of the shipyard. The fight was a desperate one, and I came out of it most shockingly mangled. I was cut and bruised in sundry places, and my left eye was nearly knocked out of its socket. The facts, leading to this barbarous outrage upon me, illustrate a phase of slavery destined to become an important element in the overthrow of the slave system, and I may, therefore state them with some minuteness. That phase is this: the conflict of slavery with the interests of the white mechanics and laborers of the south. In the country, this conflict is not so apparent; but, in cities, such as Baltimore, Richmond, New Orleans, Mobile, etc, it is seen pretty clearly. The slaveholders, with a craftiness peculiar to themselves, by encouraging the enmity of the poor, laboring white man against the blacks, succeeds in making the said white man almost as much a slave as the black slave himself. The difference between the white slave, and the black slave, is this: the latter belongs to one slaveholder, and the former belongs to all the slaveholders, collectively. The white slave has taken from him, by indirection, what the black slave has taken from him, directly, and without ceremony. Both are plundered, and by the same plunderers. The slave is robbed, by his master, of all his earnings, above what is required for his bare physical necessities; and the white man is robbed by the slave system, of the just results of his labor, because he is flung into competition with a class of laborers who work without wages. The competition, and its injurious consequences, will, one day, array the nonslaveholding white people of the slave states, against the slave system, and make them the most effective workers against the great evil.

In the city of Baltimore, there are not unfrequent murmurs, that educating the slaves to be mechanics may, in the end, give slavemasters power to dispense with the services of the poor white man altogether. But, with characteristic dread of offending the slaveholders, these poor, white mechanics in Mr. Gardiner's shipyard—instead of applying the natural, honest remedy for the apprehended evil, and objecting at once to work there by the side of slaves—made a cowardly attack upon the free colored mechanics, saying they were eating the bread which should be eaten by American freemen, and swearing that they would not work with them. The feeling was, really, against having their labor brought into competition with that of the colored people at all; but it was too much to strike directly at the interest of the slaveholders; and, therefore proving their servility and cowardice they dealt their blows on the poor, colored freeman, and aimed to prevent him from serving himself in the evening of life, with the trade with which he had served his master during the more vigorous portion of his days. Had they succeeded in driving the black freemen out of the shipyard, they would have determined also upon the removal of the black slaves. The feeling was very bitter toward all colored people in Baltimore, about this time (1836), and they—free and slave suffered all manner of insult and wrong.

Until a very little before I went there, white and black ship carpenters worked side by side, in the shipyards of Mr. Gardiner, Mr. Duncan, Mr. Walter Price, and Mr. Robb. Nobody seemed to see any impropriety in it. To outward seeming, all hands were well satisfied. Some of the blacks were first rate workmen, and were given jobs requiring highest skill. All at once, however, the white carpenters knocked off, and swore that they would no longer work on the same stage with free Negroes. Taking advantage of the heavy contract resting upon Mr. Gardiner, to have the war vessels for Mexico ready to launch in July, and of the difficulty of getting other hands at that season of the year, they swore they would not strike another blow for him, unless he would discharge his free colored workmen.

Now, although this movement did not extend to me, in form, it did reach me, in fact. The spirit which it awakened was one of malice and bitterness toward colored people generally, and I suffered with the rest, and suffered severely. My fellow apprentices very soon began to feel it to be degrading to work with me. They began to put on high looks, and to talk contemptuously and maliciously of "the Niggers;" saying, that "they would take the country," that "they ought to be killed." Encouraged by the cowardly workmen, who, knowing me to be a slave, made no issue with Mr. Gardiner about my being there, these young men did their utmost to make it impossible for me to stay. They seldom called me to do anything, without coupling the call with a curse, and Edward North, the biggest in every thing, rascality included, ventured to strike me, whereupon I picked him up, and threw him into the dock. Whenever any of them struck me, I struck back again, regardless of consequences. I could manage any of them singly, and, while I could keep them from combining, I succeeded very well. In the conflict which ended my stay at Mr. Gardiner's, I was beset by four of them at once—Ned North, Ned Hays, Bill Stewart, and Tom Humphreys. Two of them were as large as myself, and they came near killing me, in broad day light. The attack was made suddenly, and simultaneously. One came in front, armed with a brick; there was one at each side, and one behind, and they closed up around me. I was struck on all sides; and, while I was attending to those in front, I received a blow on my head, from behind, dealt with a heavy handspike. I was completely stunned by the blow, and fell, heavily, on the ground, among the timbers. Taking advantage of my fall, they rushed upon me, and began to pound me with their fists. I let them lay on, for a while, after I came to myself, with a view of gaining strength. They did me little damage, so far; but, finally, getting tired of that sport, I gave a sudden surge, and, despite their weight, I rose to my hands and knees. Just as I did this, one of their number (I know not which) planted a blow with his boot in my left eye, which, for a time, seemed to have burst my eyeball. When they saw my eye completely closed, my face covered with blood, and I staggering under the stunning blows they had given me, they left me. As soon as I gathered sufficient strength, I picked up the hand-spike, and, madly enough, attempted to pursue them; but here the carpenters interfered, and compelled me to give up my frenzied pursuit. It was impossible to stand against so many.

Dear reader, you can hardly believe the statement, but it is true, and, therefore, I write it down: not fewer than fifty white men stood by, and saw this brutal and shameless outrage committed, and not a man of them all interposed a single word of mercy. There were four against one, and that one's face was beaten and battered most horribly, and no one said, "that is enough;" but some cried out, "Kill him—kill him—kill the d—d nigger! knock his brains out—he struck a white person." I mention this inhuman outcry, to show the character of the men, and the spirit of the times, at Gardiner's shipyard, and, indeed, in Baltimore generally, in 1836. As I look back to this period, I am almost amazed that I was not murdered outright, in that shipyard, so murderous was the spirit which prevailed there.

On two occasions, while there, I came near losing my life. I was driving bolts in the hold, through the keelson with Hays. In its course, the bolt bent. Hays cursed me, and said that it was my blow which bent the bolt. I denied this, and charged it upon him. In a fit of rage he seized an adze, and darted toward me. I met him with a maul, and parried his blow, or I should have then lost my life. A son of old Tom Lanman, in the spirit of his miserable father, made an assault upon me, but the blow with his maul missed me. After the united assault of North, Stewart, Hays and Humphreys, finding that the carpenters were as bitter toward me as the apprentices, I found my only chances for life was in flight. I succeeded in getting away, without an additional blow. To strike a white man was death, by Lynch law, in Gardiner's shipyard; nor was there much of any other law toward colored people, at that time, in any other part of Maryland. The whole sentiment of Baltimore was murderous.

After making my escape from the shipyard, I went straight home, and related the story of the outrage to Master Hugh Auld; and it is due to him to say, that his conduct—though he was not a religious man—was every way more humane than that of his brother, Thomas, when I went to the latter in a somewhat similar plight, from the hands of "Brother Edward Covey." He listened attentively to my narration of the circumstances leading to the ruffianly outrage, and gave many proofs of his strong indignation at what was done. Hugh was a rough, but manly-hearted fellow, and, at this time, his best nature showed itself.

The heart of my once almost over-kind mistress, Sophia, was again melted in pity toward me. My puffed-out eye, and my scarred and blood-covered face, moved the dear lady to tears. She kindly drew a chair by me, and with friendly, consoling words, she took water, and washed the blood from my face. No mother's hand could have been more tender than hers. She bound up my head, and covered my wounded eye with a lean piece of fresh beef. It was almost compensation for the murderous assault, and my suffering, that it furnished and occasion for the manifestation, once more, of the originally characteristic kindness of my mistress. Her affectionate heart was not yet dead, though much hardened by time and by circumstances.

As for Master Hugh's part, as I have said, he was furious about it; and he gave expression to his fury in the usual forms of speech in that locality. He poured curses on the heads of the whole shipyard company, and swore that he would have satis- faction for the outrage. His indignation was really strong and healthy; but, unfortunately, it resulted from the thought that his rights of property, in my person, had not been respected, more than from any sense of the outrage committed on me as a man. I inferred as much as this, from the fact that he could, himself, beat and mangle when it suited him to do so. Bent on having satisfaction, as he said, just as soon as I got a little the better of my bruises, Master Hugh took me to Esquire Watson's office, on Bond street, Fell's Point, with a view to procuring the arrest of those who had assaulted me. He related the outrage to the magistrate, as I had related it to him, and seemed to expect that a warrant would, at once, be issued for the arrest of the lawless ruffians.

Mr. Watson heard it all, and instead of drawing up his warrant, he inquired.—
"Mr. Auld, who saw this assault of which you speak?"
"It was done, sir, in the presence of a shipyard full of hands."
"Sir," said Watson, "I am sorry, but I cannot move in this matter except upon the oath of white witnesses."
"But here's the boy; look at his head and face," said the excited Master Hugh; "they show what has been done."

But Watson insisted that he was not authorized to do anything, unless white witnesses of the transaction would come forward, and testify to what had taken place. He could issue no warrant on my word, against white persons; and, if I had been killed in the presence of a thousand blacks, their testimony, combined would have been insufficient to arrest a single murderer. Master Hugh, for once, was compelled to say, that this state of things was too bad; and he left the office of the magistrate, disgusted.

Of course, it was impossible to get any white man to testify against my assailants. The carpenters saw what was done; but the actors were but the agents of their malice, and only what the carpenters sanctioned. They had cried, with one accord, "Kill the nigger!" "Kill the nigger!" Even those who may have pitied me, if any such were among them, lacked the moral courage to come and volunteer their evidence. The slightest manifestation of sympathy or justice toward a person of color was denounced as abolitionism; and the name of abolitionist subjected its bearer to frightful liabilities. "D—n abolitionists," and "Kill the niggers," were the watchwords of the foul-mouthed ruffians of those days. Nothing was done, and probably there would not have been anything done, had I been killed in the affray. The laws and the morals of the Christian city of Baltimore, afforded no protection to the sable denizens of that city.

Master Hugh, on finding he could get no redress for the cruel wrong, withdrew me from the employment of Mr. Gardiner, and took me into his own family, Mrs. Auld kindly taking care of me, and dressing my wounds, until they were healed, and I was ready to go again to work.

While I was on the Eastern Shore, Master Hugh had met with reverses, which overthrew his business; and he had given up ship building in his own yard on the City Block, and was now acting as foreman of Mr. Walter Price. The best he could now do for me was to take me into Mr. Price's yard, and afford me the facilities there, for completing the trade which I had began to learn at Gardiner's. Here I rapidly became expert in the use of my calking tools; and, in the course of a single year, I was able to command the highest wages paid to journeymen calkers in Baltimore.

The reader will observe that I was now of some pecuniary value to my master. During the busy season, I was bringing six and seven dollars per week. I have, sometimes, brought him as much as nine dollars a week, for the wages were a dollar and a half per day.

After learning to calk, I sought my own employment, made my own contracts, and collected my own earnings; giving Master Hugh no trouble in any part of the transactions to which I was a party. Here, then, were better days for the Eastern Shore slave. I was now free from the vexatious assaults of the apprentices at Mr. Gardiner's; and free from the perils of plantation life, and once more in a favorable condition to increase my little stock of education, which had been at a dead stand since my removal from Baltimore. I had, on the Eastern Shore, been only a teacher, when in company with other slaves, but now there were colored persons who could instruct me. Many of the young calkers could read, write and cipher. Some of them had high notions about mental improvement; and the free ones, on Fell's Point, organized what they called the "East Baltimore Mental Improvement Society." To this society, notwithstanding it was intended that only free persons should attach themselves, I was admitted, and was, several times, assigned a prominent part in its debates. I owe much to the society of these young men.

The reader already knows enough of the ill effects of good treatment on a slave, to anticipate what was now the case in my improved condition. It was not long before I began to show signs of disquiet with slavery, and to look around for means to get out of that condition by the shortest route. I was living among free men; and was, in all respects, equal to them by nature and by attainments. Why should I be a slave? There was no reason why I should be the thrall of any man.

Besides, I was now getting—as I have said—a dollar and fifty cents per day. I contracted for it, worked for it, earned it, collected it; it was paid to me, and it was rightfully my own; and yet, upon every returning Saturday night, this money—my own hard earnings, every cent of it—was demanded of me, and taken from me by Master Hugh. He did not earn it; he had no hand in earning it; why, then, should he have it? I owed him nothing. He had given me no schooling, and I had received from him only my food and raiment; and for these, my services were supposed to pay, from the first. The right to take my earnings was the right of the robber. He had the power to compel me to give him the fruits of my labor, and this power was his only right in the case. I became more and more dissatisfied with this state of things; and, in so becoming, I only gave proof of the same human nature which every reader of this chapter in my life—slaveholder, or nonslaveholder—is conscious of possessing.

To make a contented slave, you must make a thoughtless one. It is necessary to darken his moral and mental vision, and, as far as possible, to annihilate his power of reason. He must be able to detect no inconsistencies in slavery. The man that takes his earnings must be able to convince him that he has a perfect right to do so. It must not depend upon mere force; the slave must know no Higher Law than his master's will. The whole relationship must not only demonstrate, to his mind, its necessity, but its absolute rightfulness. If there be one crevice through which a single drop can fall, it will certainly rust off the slave's chain.

21

The Last Straw

My condition in the year (1838) of my escape, was, comparatively, a free and easy one, so far, at least, as the wants of the physical man were concerned; but that slave life was adding nothing to its charms for me, as I grew older, and became better acquainted with it. The practice, from week to week, of openly robbing me of all my earnings, kept the nature and character of slavery constantly before me. I could be robbed by indirection, but this was too open and barefaced to be endured. I could see no reason why I should, at the end of each week, pour the reward of my honest toil into the purse of any man. The thought itself vexed me, and the manner in which Master Hugh received my wages, vexed me more than the original wrong. Carefully counting the money and rolling it out, dollar by dollar, he would look me in the face, as if he would search my heart as well as my pocket, and reproachfully ask me, "Is that all?"—implying that I had, perhaps, kept back part of my wages; or, if not so, the demand was made, possibly, to make me feel, that, after all, I was an "unprofitable servant."

Draining me of the last cent of my hard earnings, he would, however, occasionally—when I brought home an extra large sum—dole out to me a sixpence or a shilling, with a view, perhaps, of kindling up my gratitude; but this practice had the opposite effect—it was an admission of my right to the whole sum. The fact, that he gave me any part of my wages, was proof that he suspected that I had a right to the whole of them. I always felt uncomfortable, after having received anything in this way, for I feared that the giving me a few cents, might, possibly, ease his conscience, and make him feel himself a pretty honorable robber, after all!

Held to a strict account, and kept under a close watch—the old suspicion of my running away not having been entirely removed—escape from slavery, even in Baltimore, was very difficult. The railroad from Baltimore to Philadelphia was under regulations so stringent, that even free colored travelers were almost excluded. They must have free papers; they must be measured and carefully examined before they were allowed to enter the cars; they only went in the day time, even when so examined. The steamboats were under regulations equally stringent. All the great turnpikes, leading northward, were beset with kidnappers, a class of men who watched the newspapers for advertisements for runaway slaves, making their living by the accursed reward of slave hunting.

My discontent grew upon me, and I was on the look-out for means of escape. With money, I could easily have managed the matter, and, therefore, I hit upon the plan of soliciting the privilege of hiring my time. It is quite common, in Baltimore, to allow slaves this privilege, and it is the practice, also, in New Or- leans. A slave who is considered trustworthy, can, by paying his master a definite sum regularly, at the end of each week, dispose of his time as he likes. It so happened that I was not in very good odor, and I was far from being a trustworthy slave. Nevertheless, I watched my opportunity when Master Thomas came to Baltimore (for I was still his property, Hugh only acted as his agent) in the spring of 1838, to purchase his spring supply of goods, and applied to him, directly, for the much-coveted privilege of hiring my time. This request Master Thomas unhesitatingly refused to grant; and he charged me, with some sternness, with inventing this stratagem to make my escape. He told me, "I could go nowhere but he could catch me; and, in the event of my running away, I might be assured he should spare no pains in his efforts to recapture me." He recounted, with a good deal of eloquence, the many kind offices he had done me, and exhorted me to be contented and obedient. "Lay out no plans for the future," said he. "If you behave yourself properly, I will take care of you."

Now, kind and considerate as this offer was, it failed to soothe me into repose. In spite of Master Thomas, and, I may say, in spite of myself, also, I continued to think, and worse still, to think almost exclusively about the injustice and wickedness of slavery. No effort of mine or of his could silence this trouble-giving thought, or change my purpose to run away.

About two months after applying to Master Thomas for the privilege of hiring my time, I applied to Master Hugh for the same liberty, supposing him to be unacquainted with the fact that I had made a similar application to Master Thomas, and had been refused. My boldness in making this request, fairly astounded him at the first. He gazed at me in amazement. But I had many good reasons for pressing the matter; and, after listening to them awhile, he did not absolutely refuse, but told me he would think of it. Here, then, was a gleam of hope. Once master of my own time, I felt sure that I could make, over and above my obligation to him, a dollar or two every week. Some slaves have made enough, in this way, to purchase their freedom. It is a sharp spur to industry; and some of the most enterprising colored men in Baltimore hire themselves in this way.

After mature reflection—as I must suppose it was— Master Hugh granted me the privilege in question, on the following terms: I was to be allowed all my time; to make all bargains for work; to find my own employment, and to collect my own wages; and, in return for this liberty, I was required, or obliged, to pay him three dollars at the end of each week, and to board and clothe myself, and buy my own calking tools. A failure in any of these particulars would put an end to my privilege. This was a hard bargain. The wear and tear of clothing, the losing and breaking of tools, and the expense of board, made it necessary for me to earn at least six dollars per week, to keep even with the world. All who are acquainted with calking, know how uncertain and irregular that employment is. It can be done to advantage only in dry weather, for it is useless to put wet oakum into a seam. Rain or shine, however, work or no work, at the end of each week the money must be forthcoming.

Master Hugh seemed to be very much pleased, for a time, with this arrangement; and well he might be, for it was decidedly in his favor. It relieved him of all anxiety concerning me. His money was sure. He had armed my love of liberty with a lash and a driver, far more efficient than any I had before known; and, while he derived all the benefits of slaveholding by the arrangement, without its evils, I endured all the evils of being a slave, and yet suffered all the care and anxiety of a responsible freeman.

"Nevertheless," thought I, "it is a valuable privilege another step in my career toward freedom." It was something even to be permitted to stagger under the disadvantages of liberty, and I was determined to hold on to the newly gained footing, by all proper industry. I was ready to work by night as well as by day; and being in the enjoyment of excellent health, I was able not only to meet my current expenses, but also to lay by a small sum at the end of each week. All went on thus, from the month of May till August; then—for reasons which will become apparent as I proceed—my much valued liberty was wrested from me.

During the week previous to this calamitous event, I had made arrangements with a few young friends, to accompany them, on Saturday night, to a camp-meeting, held about twelve miles from Baltimore. On the evening of our intended start for the camp-ground, something occurred in the shipyard where I was at work, which detained me unusually late, and compelled me either to disappoint my young friends, or to neglect carrying my weekly dues to Master Hugh. Knowing that I had the money, and could hand it to him on another day, I decided to go to camp-meeting, and to pay him the three dollars, for the past week, on my return. Once on the camp-ground, I was induced to remain one day longer than I had intended, when I left home. But, as soon as I returned, I went straight to his house on Fell street, to hand him his (my) money. Unhappily, the fatal mistake had been committed. I found him exceedingly angry. He exhibited all the signs of apprehension and wrath which a slaveholder may be surmised to exhibit on the supposed escape of a favorite slave.

"You rascal! I have a great mind to give you a severe whipping. How dare you go out of the city without first asking and obtaining my permission?"
"Sir," said I, "I hired my time and paid you the price you asked for it. I did not know that it was any part of the bargain that I should ask you when or where I should go."
"You did not know, you rascal! You are bound to show yourself here every Saturday night."

After reflecting, a few moments, he became somewhat cooled down; but, evidently greatly troubled, he said, "Now, you scoundrel! you have done for yourself; you shall hire your time no longer. The next thing I shall hear of, will be your running away. Bring home your tools and your clothes, at once. I'll teach you how to go off in this way."

Thus ended my partial freedom. I could hire my time no longer; and I obeyed my master's orders at once. The little taste of liberty which I had had by no means enhanced my contentment with slavery. Punished thus by

Master Hugh, it was now my turn to punish him. "Since," thought I, "you will make a slave of me, I will await your orders in all things;" and, instead of going to look for work on Monday morning, as I had formerly done, I remained at home during the entire week, without the performance of a single stroke of work. Saturday night came, and he called upon me, as usual, for my wages. I, of course, told him I had done no work, and had no wages. Here we were at the point of coming to blows. His wrath had been accumulating during the whole week; for he evidently saw that I was making no effort to get work, but was most aggravatingly awaiting his orders, in all things. As I look back to this behavior of mine, I scarcely know what possessed me, thus to trifle with those who had such unlimited power to bless or to blast me.

Master Hugh raved and swore his determination to "get hold of me;" but, wisely for him, and happily for me, his wrath only employed those very harmless, impalpable missiles, which roll from a limber tongue. In my desperation, I had fully made up my mind to measure strength with Master Hugh, in case he should undertake to execute his threats. I am glad there was no necessity for this; for resistance to him could not have ended so happily for me, as it did in the case of Covey. He was not a man to be safely resisted by a slave; and I freely own, that in my conduct toward him, in this instance, there was more folly than wisdom. Master Hugh closed his reproofs, by telling me that, hereafter, I need give myself no uneasiness about getting work; that he "would, himself, see to getting work for me, and enough of it, at that." This threat I confess had some terror in it; and, on thinking the matter over, during the Sunday, I resolved, not only to save him the trouble of getting me work, but that, upon the third day of September, I would attempt to make my escape from slavery.

The refusal to allow me to hire my time, therefore, hastened the period of flight. I had three weeks, now, in which to prepare for my journey.

Once resolved, I felt a certain degree of repose, and on Monday, instead of waiting for Master Hugh to seek employment for me, I was up by break of day, and off to the shipyard of Mr. Butler, on the City Block, near the drawbridge. I was a favorite with Mr. B., and, young as I was, I had served as his foreman on the float stage, at calking. Of course, I easily obtained work, and, at the end of the week—which by the way was exceedingly fine I brought Master Hugh nearly nine dollars. The effect of this mark of returning good sense, on my part, was excellent. He was very much pleased; he took the money, commended me, and told me I might have done the same thing the week before. It is a blessed thing that the tyrant may not always know the thoughts and purposes of his victim. Master Hugh little knew what my plans were. The going to camp-meeting without asking his permission—the insolent answers made to his reproaches—the sulky deportment the week after being deprived of the privilege of hiring my time—had awakened in him the suspicion that I might be cherishing disloyal purposes. My object, therefore, in working steadily, was to remove suspicion, and in this I succeeded admirably. He probably thought I was never better satisfied with my condition, than at the very time I was planning my escape.

The second week passed, and again I carried him my full week's wages—nine dollars; and so well pleased was he, that he gave me TWENTY-FIVE CENTS! and "bade me make good use of it!" I told him I would, for one of the uses to which I meant to put it, was to pay my fare on the underground railroad.

Things without went on as usual; but I was passing through the same internal excitement and anxiety which I had experienced two years and a half before. The failure, in that instance, was not calculated to increase my confidence in the success of this, my second attempt; and I knew that a second failure could not leave me where my first did—I must either get to the far north, or be sent to the far south. Besides the exercise of mind from this state of facts, I had the painful sensation of being about to separate from a circle of honest and warm hearted friends in Baltimore. The thought of such a separation, where the hope of ever meeting again is excluded, and where there can be no correspondence, is very painful. It is my opinion, that thousands would escape from slavery who now remain there, but for the strong cords of affection that bind them to their families, relatives and friends. The daughter is hindered from escaping, by the love she bears her mother, and the father, by the love he bears his children. I had no relations in Baltimore, and I saw no probability of ever living in the neighborhood of sisters and brothers; but the thought of leaving my friends was among the strongest obstacles to my running away.

The last two days of the week—Friday and Saturday—were spent mostly in collecting my things together for my journey. Having worked four days that week for my master, I handed him six dollars, on Saturday night. I seldom spent my Sundays at home; and, for fear that something might be discovered in my conduct, I kept up my custom, and absented myself all day. On Monday, the third day of September, 1838, in accordance with my resolution, I bade farewell to the city of Baltimore, and to that slavery which had been my abhorrence from childhood.

How I got away—in what direction I traveled—whether by land or by water; whether with or without assistance —must remain unexplained. I must deprive myself of the pleasure, and the curious of the gratification, to state the details and facts of my escape. The reason is simple:

The practice of publishing every new invention by which a slave is known to have escaped from slavery, has neither wisdom nor necessity to sustain it. Had not Henry Box Brown and his friends attracted slaveholding attention to the manner of his escape, we might have had a thousand Box Browns per annum. The singularly original plan adopted by William and Ellen Crafts, perished with the first using, because every slaveholder in the land was apprised of it. The salt water slave who hung in the guards of a steamer, being washed three days and three nights—like another Jonah—by the waves of the sea, has, by the publicity given to the circumstance, set a spy on the guards of every steamer departing from southern ports.

I have never approved of the very public manner in which some of our western friends have tell stories about the "Underground Railroad," which, I think, by their open declarations, has been made, most emphatically, the "Upperground Railroad." Its stations are far better known to the slaveholders than to the slaves. I honor those good men and women for their noble daring, in willingly subjecting themselves to persecution, by openly avowing their participation in the escape of slaves; nevertheless, the good resulting from such avowals (it may kindle an enthusiasm, very pleasant to inhale), is of no practical benefit to themselves, nor to the slaves escaping. In publishing such accounts, the anti-slavery man addresses the slaveholder, not the slave; he stimulates the former to greater watchfulness, and adds to his facilities for capturing his slave. We owe something to the slaves, still south of Mason and Dixon's line, as well as to those north of it; we should be careful to do nothing which would be likely to hinder them in making their escape from slavery. Such is my detestation of slavery, that I would keep the merciless slaveholder profoundly ignorant of the means of flight adopted by the slave. In pursuing his victim, let him be left to feel his way in the dark; let shades of darkness, commensurate with his crime, shut every ray of light from his pathway; and let him be made to feel, that, at every step he takes, with the hellish purpose of reducing a brother man to slavery, he is running the frightful risk of founding nothing but death to himself.

I would surely tell you reader, that the flight was a bold and perilous one; but here I am, in the great city of New York, safe and sound, without loss of blood or bone. In less than a week after leaving Baltimore, I was walking amid the hurrying throng, and gazing upon the dazzling wonders of Broadway. The dreams of my childhood and the purposes of my manhood were now fulfilled. A free state around me, and a free earth under my feet! What a moment was this to me! A whole year was pressed into a single day. A new world burst upon my agitated vision.

I have often been asked, by kind friends to whom I have told my story, how I felt when first I found myself beyond the limits of slavery; and I must say here, as I have often said to them, there is scarcely anything about which I could not give a more satis- factory answer. It was a moment of joyous excitement, which no words can describe. In a letter to a friend, written soon after reaching New York. I said I felt as one might be supposed to feel, on escaping from a den of hungry lions. But, in a moment like that, sensations are too intense and too rapid for words. Anguish and grief, like darkness and rain, may be described, but joy and gladness, like the rainbow of promise, defy alike the pen and pencil.

For ten or fifteen years I had been dragging a heavy chain, with a huge block attached to it, cumbering my every motion. I had felt myself doomed to drag this chain and this block through life. All efforts, before, to separate myself from the hateful encumbrance, had only seemed to rivet me the more firmly to it. Baffled and discouraged at times, I had asked myself the question, May not this, after all, be God's work? May He not, for wise ends, have doomed me to this lot? A contest had been going on in my mind for years, between the clear consciousness of right and the plausible errors of superstition; between the wisdom of manly courage, and the foolish weakness of timidity. The contest was now ended; the chain was severed; God and right stood vindicated.

I was A FREEMAN, and the voice of peace and joy thrilled my heart.

END OF THE NARRATIVE.

Secret Escape Revealed

Forty years after his escape, Frederick Douglass wrote an article where he indeed revealed, at last, some of the details of how he reached New York from Baltimore. It was safe now to do so, since the abolitionist's fight against slavery and the Civil War fought between the North and the South had settled the differences in opinion about the ownership of slaves. Slavery had been abolished by the time of the writing of this article, escape was no longer necessary, and the details on how to escape were safe to be published. Douglass will continue to write profusely about his experience with slavery and the individual rights of the negroes for the rest of his life. He knew that the battle was not over, since the treatment of the negro had not improved much in the deep South, were the hand of the Federal government was to short to protect them. Here now his narration of his escape:

"It was the custom in the State of Maryland to require the free colored people to have what were called free papers. These instruments they were required to renew very often, and by charging a fee for this writing, considerable sums from time to time were collected by the State. In these papers the name, age, color, height, and form of the freeman were described, together with any scars or other marks upon his person which could assist in his identification. This device in some measure defeated itself—since more than one man could be found to answer the same general description. Hence many slaves could escape by personating the owner of one set of papers; and this was often done as follows: A slave, nearly or sufficiently answering the description set forth in the papers, would borrow or hire them till by means of them he could escape to a free State, and then, by mail or otherwise, would return them to the owner.

The operation was a hazardous one for the lender as well as for the borrower. A failure on the part of the fugitive to send back the papers would imperil his benefactor, and the discovery of the papers in possession of the wrong man would imperil both the fugitive and his friend. It was, therefore, an act of supreme trust on the part of a freeman of color thus to put in jeopardy his own liberty that another might be free. It was, however, not infrequently bravely done, and was seldom discovered. I was not so fortunate as to resemble any of my free acquaintances sufficiently to answer the description of their papers. But I had a friend—a sailor—who owned a sailor's protection, which answered somewhat the purpose of free papers—describing his person, and certifying to the fact that he was a free American sailor. The instrument had at its head the American eagle, which gave it the appearance at once of an authorized document. This protection, when in my hands, did not describe its bearer very accurately. Indeed, it called for a man much darker than myself, and close examination of it would have caused my arrest at the start.

In order to avoid this fatal scrutiny on the part of railroad officials, I arranged with Isaac Rolls, a Baltimore hackman, to bring my baggage to the Philadelphia train just on the moment of starting, and jumped upon the car myself when the train was in motion. Had I gone into the station and offered to purchase a ticket, I should have been instantly and carefully examined, and undoubtedly arrested. In choosing this plan I considered the jostle of the train, and the natural haste of the conductor, in a train crowded with passengers, and relied upon my skill and address in playing the sailor, as described in my protection, to do the rest. One element in my favor was the kind feeling which prevailed in Baltimore and other sea-ports at the time, toward "those who go down to the sea in ships." "Free trade and sailors' rights" just then expressed the sentiment of the country.

In my clothing I was rigged out in sailor style. I had on a red shirt and a tarpaulin hat, and a black cravat tied in sailor fashion carelessly and loosely about my neck. My knowledge of ships and sailor's talk came much to my assistance, for I knew a ship from stem to stern, and from keelson to cross-trees, and could talk sailor like an "old salt." I was well on the way to Havre de Grace before the conductor came into the negro car to collect tickets and examine the papers of his black passengers. This was a critical moment in the drama. My whole future depended upon the decision of this conductor. Agitated though I was while this ceremony was proceeding, still, externally, at least, I was apparently calm and self-possessed. He went on with his duty—examining several colored passengers before reaching me. He was somewhat harsh in tome and peremptory in manner until he reached me, when, strange enough, and to my surprise and relief, his whole manner changed. Seeing that I did not readily produce my free papers, as the other colored persons in the car had done, he said to me, in friendly contrast with his bearing toward the others:

"I suppose you have your free papers?"

To which I answered:

"No sir; I never carry my free papers to sea with me."

"But you have something to show that you are a freeman, haven't you?"

"Yes, sir," I answered; "I have a paper with the American Eagle on it, and that will carry me around the world."

With this I drew from my deep sailor's pocket my seaman's protection, as before described. The merest glance at the paper satisfied him, and he took my fare and went on about his business. This moment of time was one of the most anxious I ever experienced. Had the conductor looked closely at the paper, he could not have failed to discover that it called for a very different-looking person from myself, and in that case it would have been his duty to arrest me on the instant, and send me back to Baltimore from the first station. When he left me with the assurance that I was all right, though much relieved, I realized that I was still in great danger: I was still in Maryland, and subject to arrest at any moment. I saw on the train several persons who would have known me in any other clothes, and I feared they might recognize me, even in my sailor "rig," and report me to the conductor, who would then subject me to a closer examination, which I knew well would be fatal to me.

Though I was not a murderer fleeing from justice, I felt perhaps quite as miserable as such a criminal. The train was moving at a very high rate of speed for that epoch of railroad travel, but to my anxious mind it was moving far too slowly. Minutes were hours, and hours were days during this part of my flight. After Maryland, I was to pass through Delaware—another slave State, where slave-catchers generally awaited their prey, for it was not in the interior of the State, but on its borders, that these human hounds were most vigilant and active. The border lines between slavery and freedom were the dangerous ones for the fugitives. The heart of no fox or deer, with hungry hounds on his trail in full chase, could have beaten more anxiously or noisily than did mine from the time I left Baltimore till I reached Philadelphia.

The passage of the Susquehanna River at Havre de Grace was at that time made by ferry-boat, on board of which I met a young colored man by the name of Nichols, who came very near betraying me. He was a "hand" on the boat, but, instead of minding his business, he insisted upon knowing me, and asking me dangerous questions as to where I was going, when I was coming back, etc. I got away from my old and inconvenient acquaintance as soon as I could decently do so, and went to another part of the boat.

Once across the river, I encountered a new danger. Only a few days before, I had been at work on a revenue cutter, in Mr. Price's shipyard in Baltimore, under the care of Captain McGowan. On the meeting at this point of the two trains, the one going south stopped on the track just opposite to the one going north, and it so happened that this Captain McGowan sat at a window where he could see me very distinctly, and would certainly have recognized me had he looked at me but for a second. Fortunately, in the hurry of the moment, he did not see me; and the trains soon passed each other on their respective ways. But this was not my only hair-breadth escape.

A German blacksmith whom I knew well was on the train with me, and looked at me very intently, as if he thought he had seen me somewhere before in his travels. I really believe he knew me, but had no heart to betray me. At any rate, he saw me escaping and held his peace.

The last point of imminent danger, and the one I dreaded most, was Wilmington. Here we left the train and took the steam-boat for Philadelphia. In making the change here I again apprehended arrest, but no one disturbed me, and I was soon on the broad and beautiful Delaware, speeding away to the Quaker City. On reaching Philadelphia in the afternoon, I inquired of a colored man how I could get on to New York. He directed me to the William-street depot, and thither I went, taking the train that night. I reached New York Tuesday morning, having completed the journey in less than twenty-four hours.

My free life began on the third of September, 1838."

DON'T MISS THE REST OF THE SERIES

VOICES OF FREEDOM

AT PADMORECULTURE.COM

www.ingramcontent.com/pod-product-compliance
Lightning Source LLC
Chambersburg PA
CBHW071602080526
44588CB00010B/993